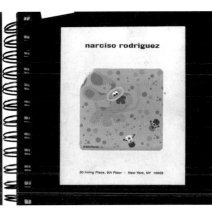

narciso rodriguez

for Carolyn

Narciso Rodriguez   by Betsy Berne

Narciso Rodriguez is not unlike an artist whose canvas is the body. Passionate about process and craft, he makes clothes that celebrate the body as well as the body in motion. The process begins with intuition or instinct or intellect—or perhaps a combination thereof. It is a fluid progression with no set beginning, middle, or end. While the process entails an exacting approach to the craft, it is predicated on a purist's aesthetic that relies on improvisation and an open attitude, allowing for the spontaneity and surprises that lead to innovation and evolution.

For Rodriguez, the aim is to convey sensuality without overt sexuality, while taking the craft—the cut, the fit, the use of new materials—to a higher level. His work is simultaneously refined, elegant, and accessible. Rodriguez creates clothing that transcends time (or, in fashion-speak, seasons): it is relevant to the way we live yet has an eye on the future. His work thrives in this "state of flux": the collections follow a natural trajectory that appears to be seamless, effortless. Not unlike the painter who arbitrarily declares a painting finished so as to move on to the next one, Rodriguez has said, "Only when the current collection has gone far enough to carry me forward to the next season is it done."

In Rodriguez's work, all aspects of life inform the process, whether conscious or not, just as his decision as an adolescent to become a designer was more unconscious than not. It was not a career choice per se, but a subliminal decision to embrace an all-consuming way of life. The son of first-generation Cuban immigrants, the designer visibly references his heritage in his work—not in the stereotypically Latin, lavishly embellished aesthetic but, culturally, through the high esteem typically held for women by Latin men. The designer shows deep respect for women as strong individuals, and an appreciation for the inherent beauty of the female form. He has spoken of being inspired by the sensuality and refined elegance of Latin people, "the pride with which they carry themselves," and of the "air of romance" that coexists with the "rawness" of Latin countries.

This same heritage has a more personal yet invisible impact on his work. Of his upbringing in Newark, New Jersey, he has written:

> **Growing up in this home instilled in me a great sense that "family" did not necessarily mean being a blood relative. Quite the contrary, our neighborhood was made up of mostly Spanish, Cuban, and Italian immigrants, and in a time when overt racism was the norm and segregation prevailed in the U.S., all of these cultures came together in great solidarity and friendship. . . . It was here where I learned the real definition of "family." For this reason I will never forget this simple house and its gracious neighborhood and everything about life and love it taught me.**

Indeed, the designer's upbringing is reflected in the small company he established initially in Milan a decade ago and subsequently in New York, beginning with just one patternmaker, one seamstress, and himself. He has since replicated his Latin parents' "community as family" tradition, creating an American stu-

dio modeled after the typical European atelier, where designer, assistants, seamstresses, patternmakers, and office personnel interact like a family. Meetings are called on a whim, meals are shared, loyalty and integrity are givens. The atmosphere is intimate and informal. Collaboration flows with an air of nonchalance and ease, the ambience reminiscent of avant-garde jazz, a play of lyrical improvisation among members who need little rehearsal, culminating in predictably unpredictable results.

Rodriguez is interested in fashion that is approachable—his garments are meant to be worn in all walks of life. Unlike designers that use separate design teams to create distinct runway and selling collections, he does not create looks solely for the catwalk. Following the true American tradition of fashion, his runway collection goes straight to the women and men who wear the clothing.

Rodriguez's inspiration is derived from the energy of urban life: the daily clash of intimate drama and banal ritual; the dichotomy between the intricate sidewalk dance of crowds moving from point A to B and a single body in motion on the dance floor; the twenty-four-hour infrastructure of a New York City that functions with keen intelligence against a streetwise culture doing its best to disrupt. References from art, music, film, and architecture all come into play, but fashion references do not. While Rodriguez deeply admires such iconic designers as Chanel or Balenciaga, he prefers to "look back in reverence, not reference." As for architecture, literal elements may contribute to a garment's structure, but it still serves primarily as a source of beauty, comfort, and longevity.

Rodriguez's major architectural influences are eclectic and often paradoxical, ranging from the deceptively simple elegance of Mies van der Rohe's work to the fantastic otherworldly architecture of Oscar Niemeyer. References from other visual arts may be specific or abstract: a season's palette may be inspired by Anish Kapoor's pigment-saturated biomorphic prints or a new cut influenced by the stark poetry of the Russian Constructivists. Fabric and pattern may be inspired by the patina of Richard Serra's majestic forms or the lush surfaces of Gerhard Richter's paintings. Music, of course, is an underlying omnipresence in Rodriguez's work, reflected in the color, pattern, silhouette, and visual rhythms that echo between design elements.

Equally significant are the notebooks that accompany the designer as he moves through the city, an eyewitness to its energy, wit, and spirit, surveying the panorama from every angle, through every transition. Rodriguez is an exceptional virtuosic draftsman; his sketches embrace the ferocity and sensuality of de Kooning's women and the kinetic energy of Giacometti's long, lean figures. Ideas are "recorded" while on the move, through "character" or "thought" sketches that convey the velocity of the subway, the speed of running on a treadmill, or the more relaxed pace of strolling in the city's parks. Conversely, the drawings strive to catch the city and its people at a standstill, during moments of rest and renewal.

The camera serves as another important visual tool as Rodriguez captures the city from dawn to dusk. The measured quietude of a cityscape asleep is photographed from the designer's apartment high above. Down below, the camera takes on the street scene: the disparate energies of the sidewalks and the subways, the parks and the promenades, people on their way to work and back home again at twilight, returning in the ambiguous light between day and night; teens going to and from school, hanging out in the afternoons, heading out to the clubs at nightfall. A passer-by's choice of dress—an insouciance, a certain poise, an air of invincibility, a graceful movement—any of these could seize the designer's imagination and influence the proportion—or tone or palette—of an entire collection.

Moving seamlessly from cityscape to landscape, Rodriguez takes pictures from a car speeding along the bumpy back roads of his beloved Brazil. A rainbow of houses painted sky blue, green, pink, and pale violet refines a new season's palette. Kites being flown on the beach suggest the sensuality and fluidity of a woman's body. A repetitive grid of mottled sand formations is transformed into a shimmer of graphic translucence; swirls of beaded embroidery become a simple sheath dress.

In the studio, Rodriguez balances a classic hands-on approach to design with a distinctive modern sensibility. His approach is essentially straightforward and traditional. In the words of the designer: "I choose my fabrics, think about what I want to make, how I want to make it; sketch it, pin fabric to the sketch, put it on the wall and send it down the runway." In reality, the process is more serendipitous, grounded in a point of view that is unwavering yet always evolving, a modern logic infused with play.

The initial phase is solitary, a form of internal free association often determined by external stimuli. Ideas germinate and collide, come together or pull apart, until a play of opposing forces begins to coalesce, triggering the first seed of a new collection for the coming season.

The sketches and photos that comprise the season's key inspirations converge as a tangible visual mindscape known as the "inspiration wall." It is a collage of visual reminders and cues that appear, at first glance, to be completely unrelated: football teams going at one another, a single cougar poised to attack, a ballerina mid-jump, a shadow alluding to a figure, a crowd of club kids, a suspension bridge. After another glance, the board appears to describe the nature of duality. Then finally the board makes perfect sense. It is a musical score that is visual, a composition of contrasting elements that describe some property of the human body: something as simple as the body's fundamental grace and beauty or as complex as how we move through space. Ultimately one of the elements on the wall will trigger a thought process, and a new collection takes off. Often it is one essential idea that has been evolving for the last decade and hasn't been realized yet. It might be the physical properties of a new material informed by technology, a seam that didn't quite work out last season that finally makes sense, or the engineering behind a suspension bridge. The springboard may be plucked from the piles of snapshots laid out on the long table in Rodriguez's studio. A series of photos of backs might become transformed literally or translated anew: a club kid at a deli wearing suspenders inspires a slender crisscross of straps; shadows from a leafy tree create amorphous shapes on a woman's back, which in turn become a beaded embellishment on a simple sheath; the shadowy grid of scaffolding is echoed on another woman's back, which translates into the signature cutouts on the back of a sleek evening gown's bodice.

In another group of photos from the same series, figures on the street are observed from behind. The pictures look quite ordinary at first. The figures are dressed casually, wearing big coats or hooded sweatshirts with jeans; they're carrying big purses or hauling backpacks. Upon closer inspection, the viewer begins to notice a relationship between details in the surrounding cityscape: elongated shadows that bisect the sidewalk, a pattern of broad white stripes, the glittering metallic surface. These everyday details of industrial design are reinterpreted by Rodriguez to become new silhouettes, constructions, shapes, and patterns. At times the designer will simply begin playing with scraps of fabric, placing one against another until a graphic collage forms. One collage will lead to another until there is an entire board of raw silhouettes or "fabric sketches"—fabric duets that produce a symphony of color and shape that serves as a road map for the runway.

Like every genuine artist or musician, Rodriguez relies on deliberate actions to provoke "mistakes," culminating in a shifting balance of the purposeful and the unexpected. The linear progression that follows is infused with equal parts logic and instinct. For the Fall 2007 collection, Rodriguez was initially inspired by Thomas Ruff's images of ambiguous sexual acts; what the images left to the imagination triggered the thought process. Car parts provided another inspiration for the same collection, leading to the creation of body molds and breastplates made of fiberglass. In short, what may seem inexplicable is simply the work of a visionary eye, a vast amount of knowledge about and experience with the craft, and a highly sophisticated visual imagination.

According to Rodriguez, he "designs in the classic sense." He follows a personal approach to design, with the goal of providing a frame to enhance, not overwhelm, an individual's person and personality. While often described as a minimalist, the designer prefers the term *purist*. Nothing extraneous exists on a garment; if there is some form of embellishment used, it is the result of the construction process. Rodriguez designs from the inside out; the inner structure of a garment is as important as the outside in terms of the way it looks and functions. It has been said that Rodriguez "doesn't see things flat, he sees in 3D—back, front, and the side." Indeed the designer often drapes directly on the model. He has said that one detail can determine a fit. He works with real bodies in an effort to discover that singular detail, searching for the precise location of the seam, making multiple barely discernible adjustments through draping and re-draping, marking and re-marking. While the work defines itself by "fit, fabric, and finish," Rodriguez is driven most of all by his love of the craft. His passion is to achieve an eloquent sensuality that is above all about movement: "the way a woman moves, the way a man carries himself,

the sway of hips, the curve of the back, the nape of the neck."
The colors black and white have always been a strong constant in the designer's work. "There is a singular graphic element to black while white embodies a purity; when used together they create a tension. They're both very rich; there are hundreds of different blacks and whites." While this may suggest the use of a limited palette, the opposite is true. Rodriguez is a truly original colorist with a discerning eye. His work has always been informed by a nuanced yet select palette, and in recent years his range has become more expansive and eclectic.

In 2006, he inaugurated the men's collection. This small, highly focused collection was a natural evolution based on logic and the right timing—and, according to the designer, some leftover fabric from a women's collection that he decided would be well suited for menswear. In fact, his fit for women was originally inspired by menswear. According to the designer: "Doing menswear is to come full circle, like retracing, editing where I've come from." The goal is to discover new ways to construct and reinvent classic menswear, to create clothing that feels good, fits well, and functions. Well-considered, almost imperceptible details, like an extra seam on the back and front of pant legs or a crucial seam across the chest, have already become signature elements. Just as menswear has informed womenswear for the past decade, womenswear now informs menswear, while the same dualities—elegance and sensuality, strength and vulnerability—and the same logic inform both. All aspects of Rodriguez's work are characterized by the concept of duality: ambiguity and unerring precison, the romantic and the rational, beauty and logic, rawness and refinement, the interior structure of a garment versus the exterior, the back versus the front. His training also embraces this duality. According to the designer, his spirit and creativity come from his experience in European ateliers, while working with American sportswear icons Calvin Klein and Donna Karan taught him about the practical side of fashion and the importance of creating clothes that are wearable. Yet Rodriguez considers himself neither an American designer nor a global designer. He says that he is a designer, period. He has no interest in the ubiquitous term "global." For Rodriguez, there are no borders in design: "Design is much more personal and comes from the hand—not from image-branding or advertising. What I'm interested in is design that touches people's lives and functions in people's lives." Nonetheless, there is no question that Rodriguez has dispensed with the boundaries of universal fashion, and in doing so has redefined American style. Narciso Rodriguez creates collections that evolve as organically as the seasons change, yet he makes classical modern clothing that is seasonless, that functions both practically and aesthetically, and, most important, is designed for seasons to come. His work is derived from a singular vision inspired by a personal history and influenced by the culture of the present; it captures the moment while alluding to what is next. Just as Rodriguez's body of work exists in a perpetual state of flux, a single Narciso Rodriguez garment captures the never-static nature of the body as an object of eternal beauty and grace.

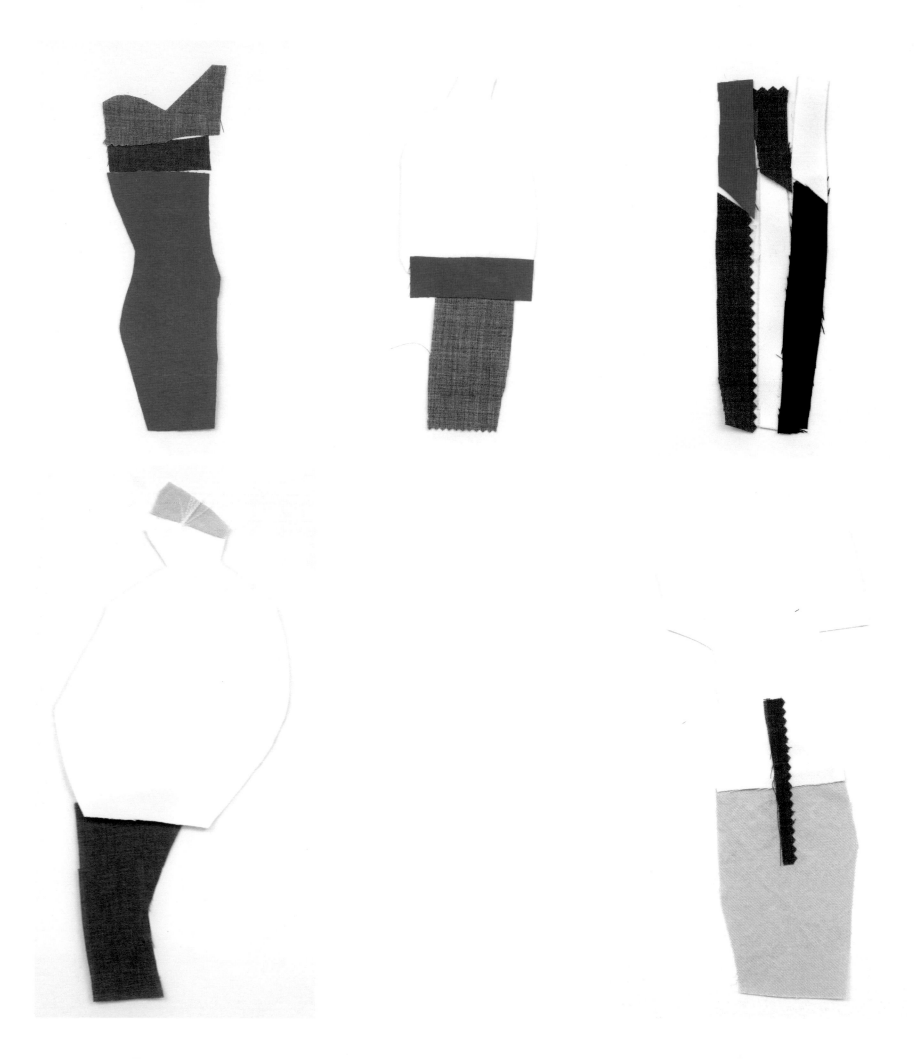

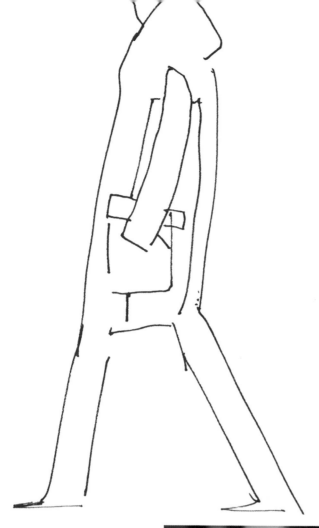

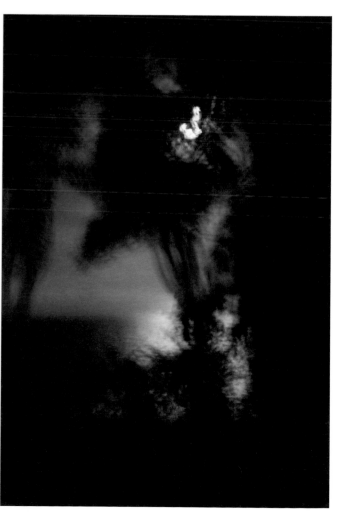

reverse

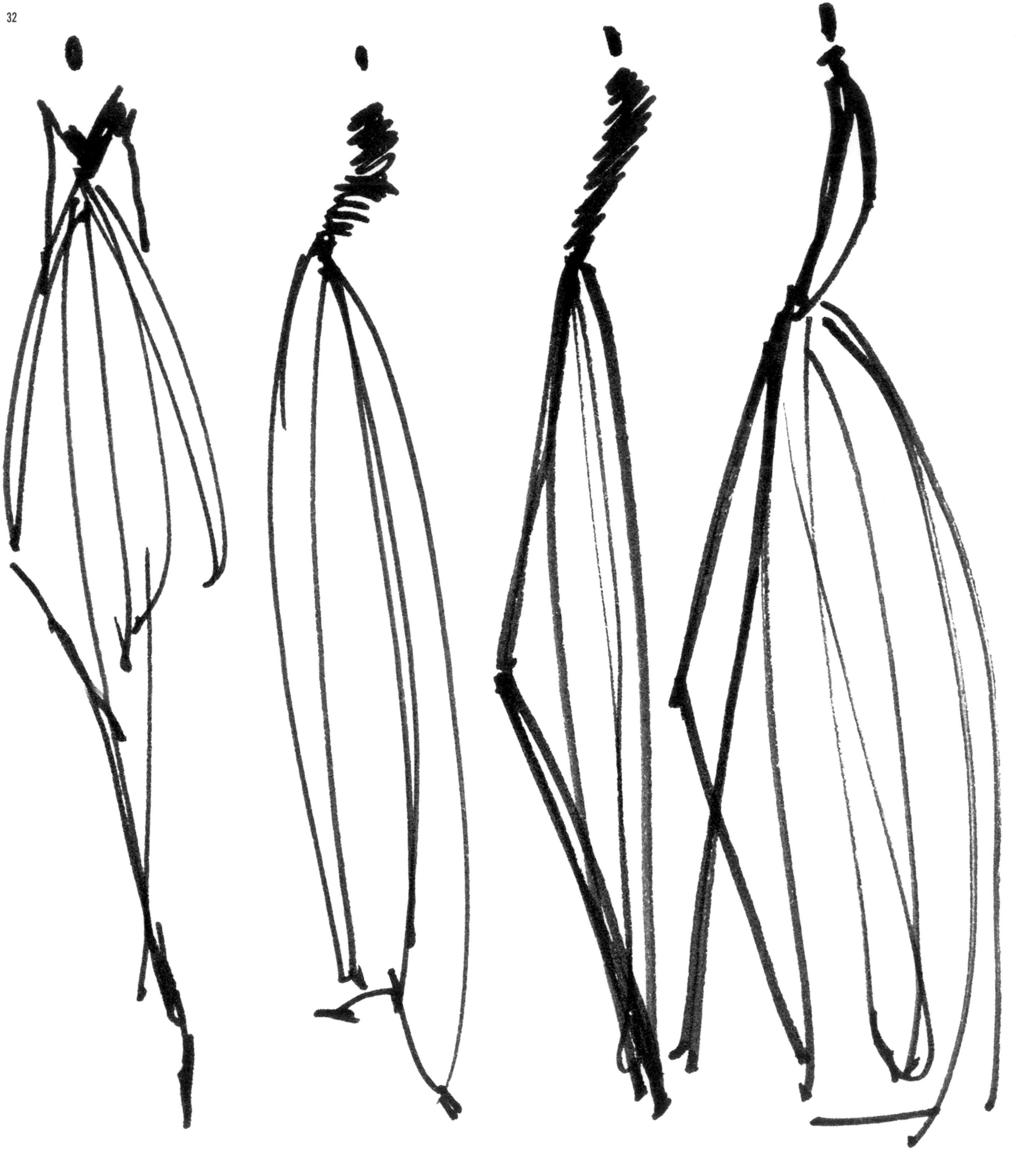

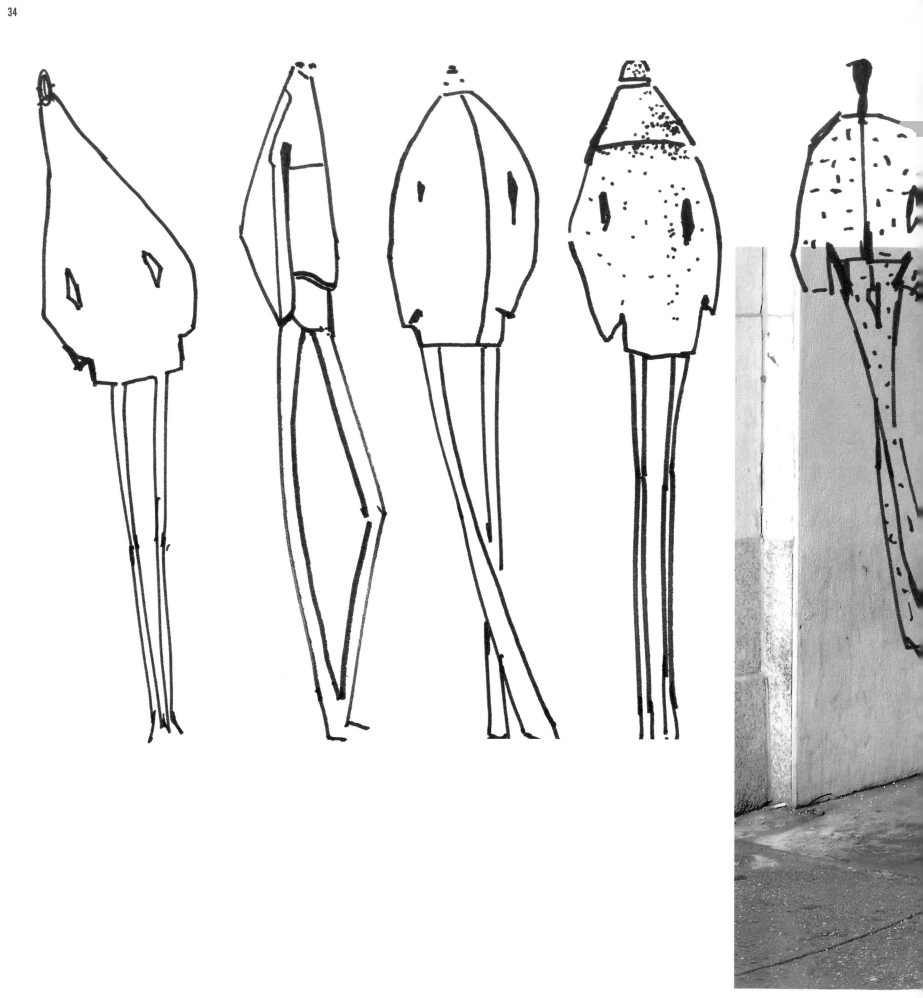

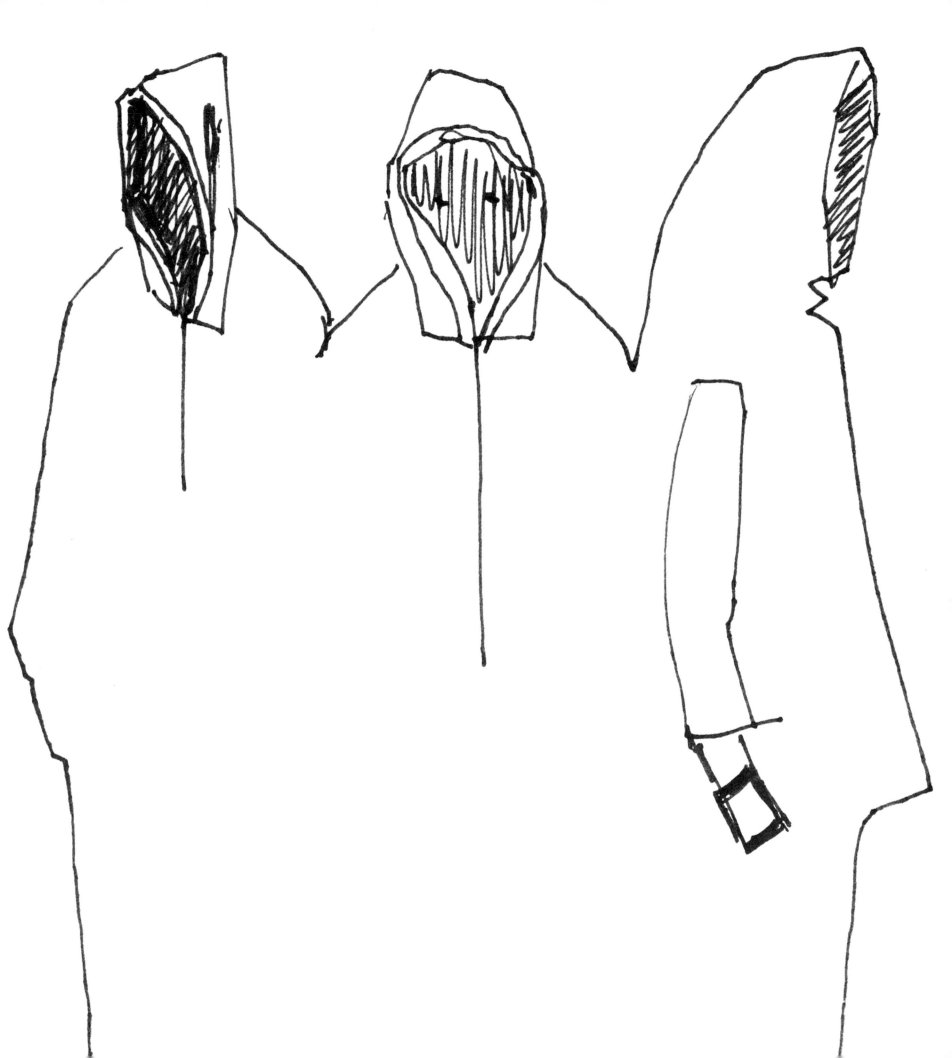

Diese Seite: Dunkelblauer Kurzmantel mit goldfarbenen Knöp-
fen, um 1130 €, von FAY. Silber-
weißes Hemd, schwarze Hose
und Slipper, alles von CHLOÉ.
Linke Seite: Schwarzer doppel-
reihiger Kurzmantel mit Lack-
applikationen an Taschen und
Kragen, um 1240 €, und schwarze
Leggings, beides von VERSACE.
Auf diesen und den vorhergehen-
den 12 Seiten: Frisuren von Seb
Bascle. Make-up: Lili Choi, beide
für Blunt, mit Produkten von
MAC. Moderedakteur: Nicola
Knels. Assistenz: Alice Eikelpoth.
„VOGUE Adressen": ab Seite 226.

205

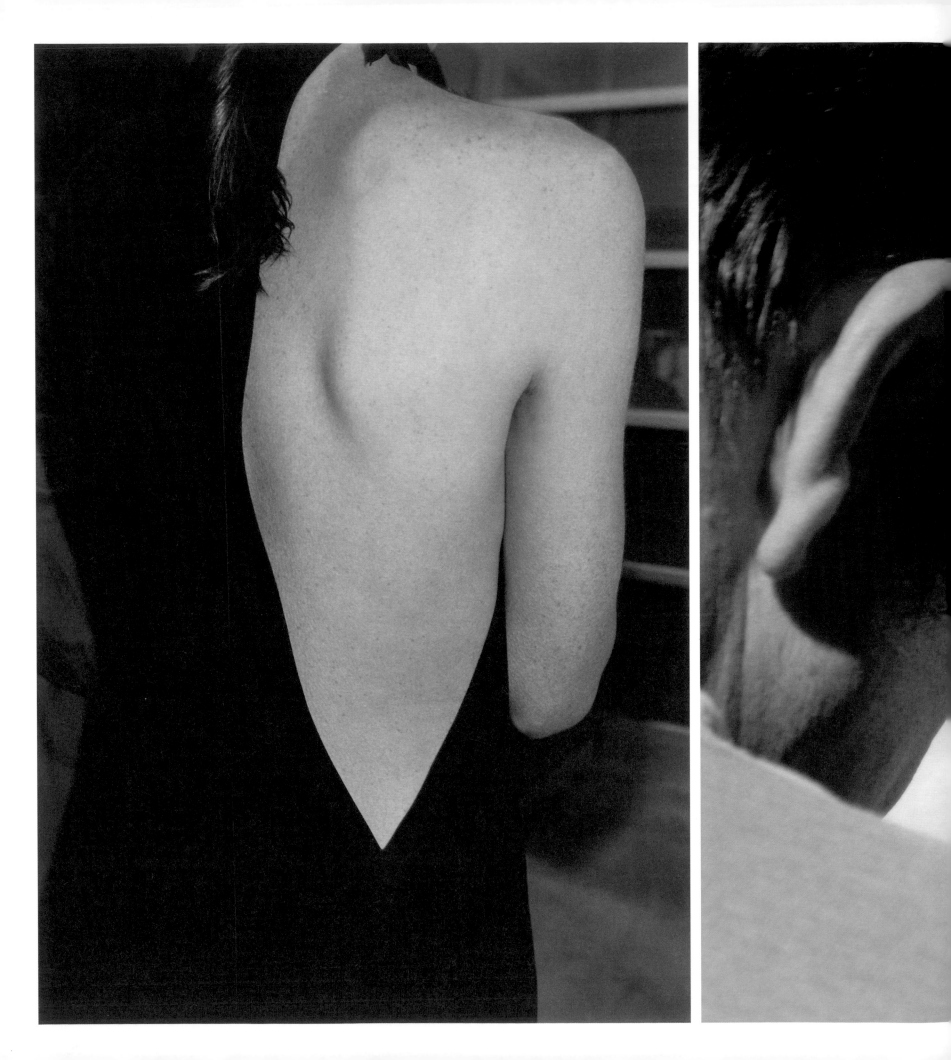

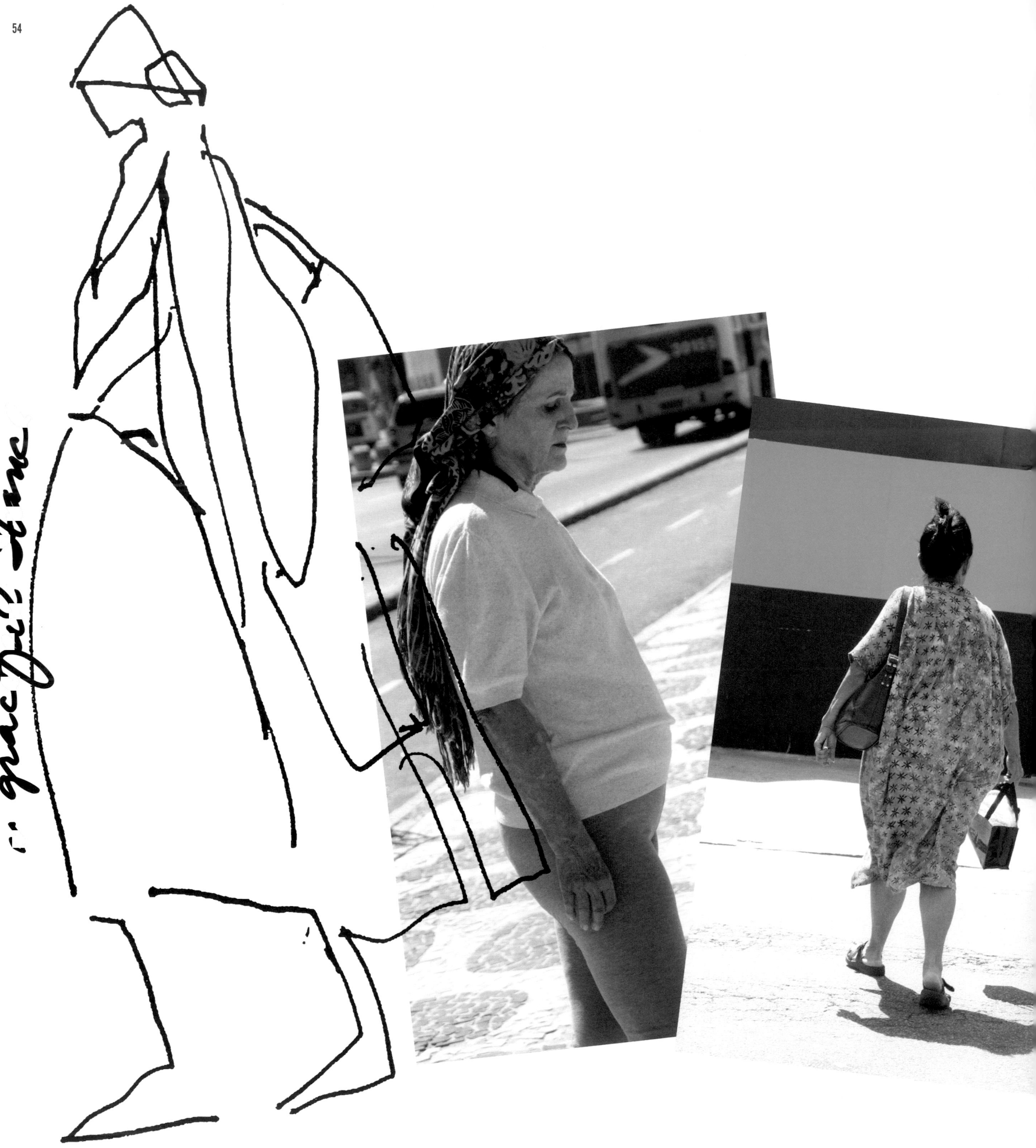

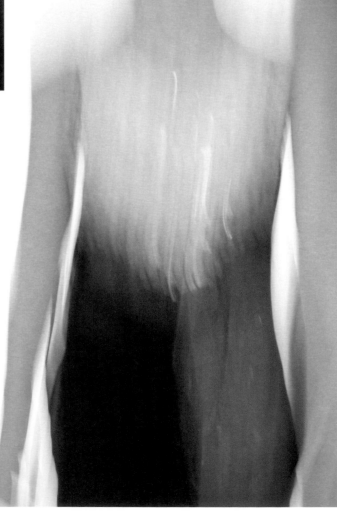

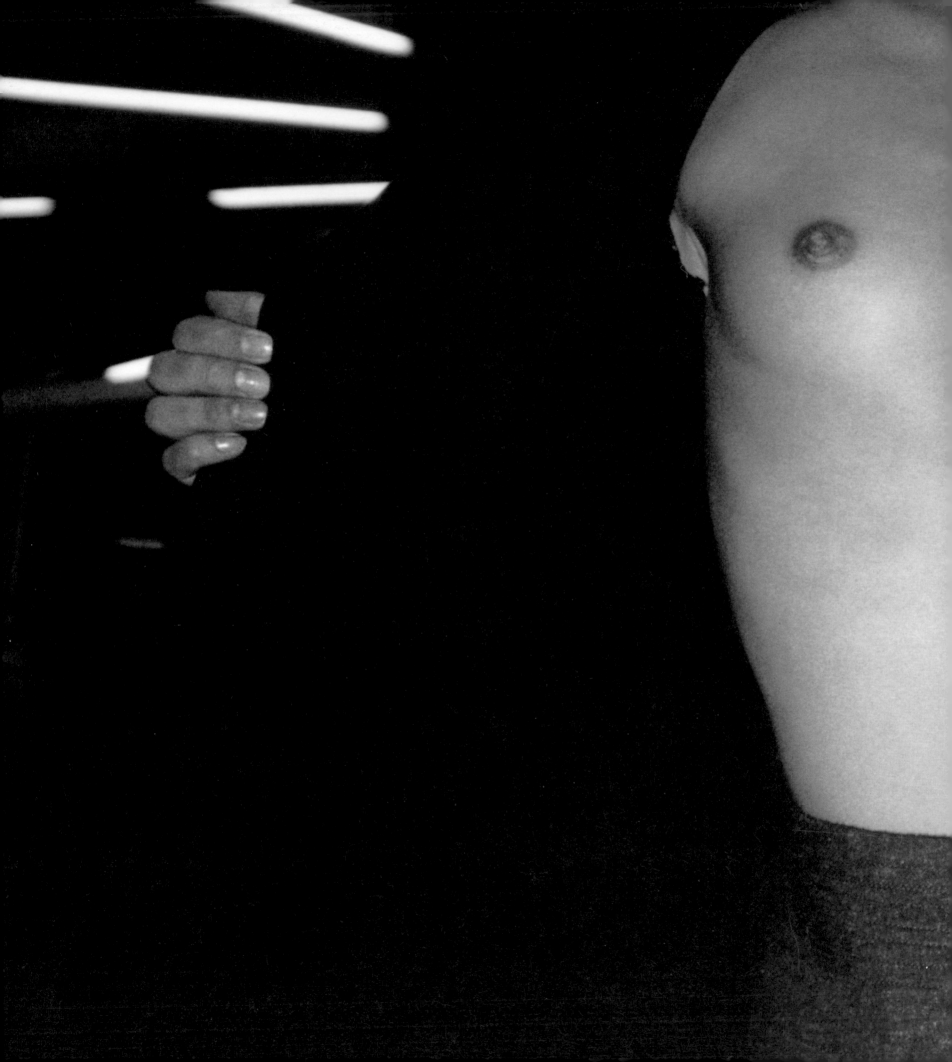

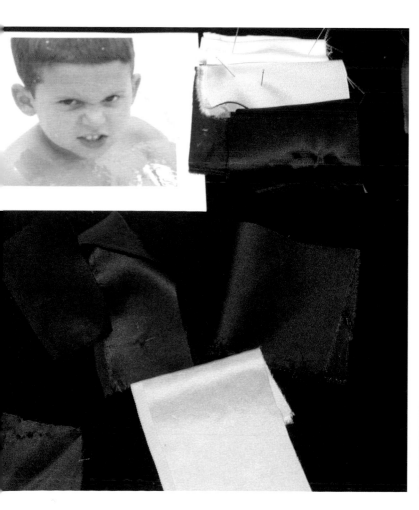

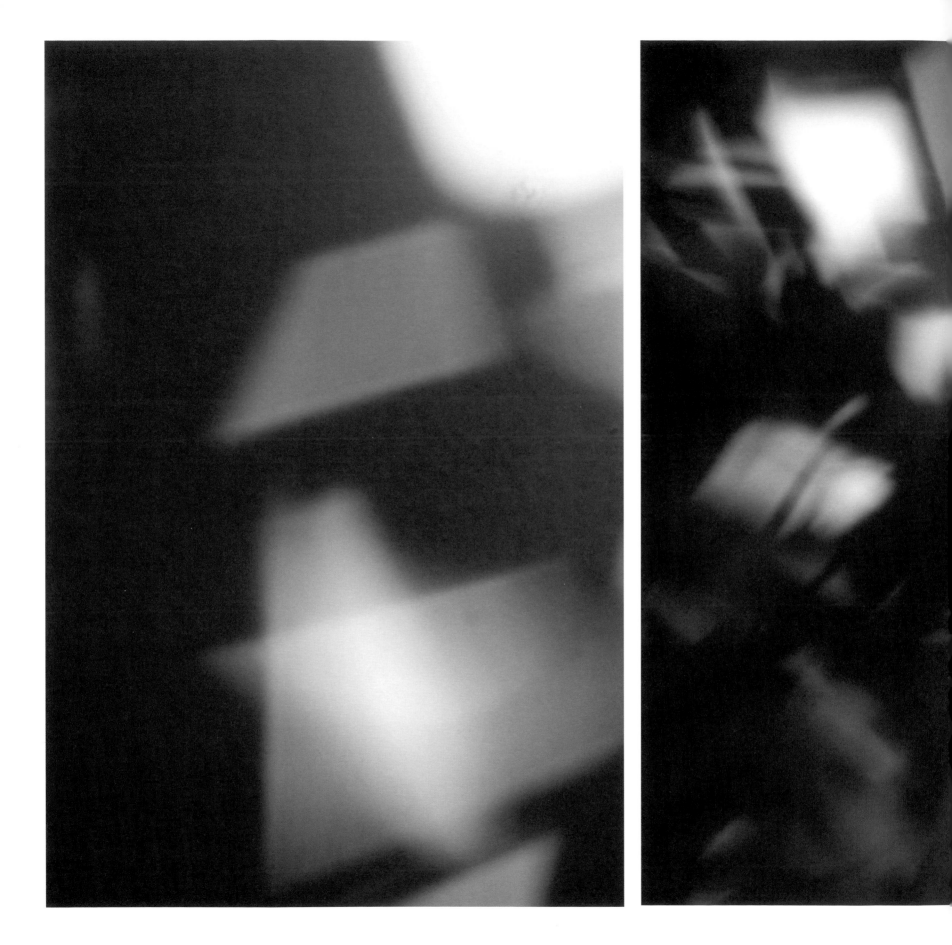

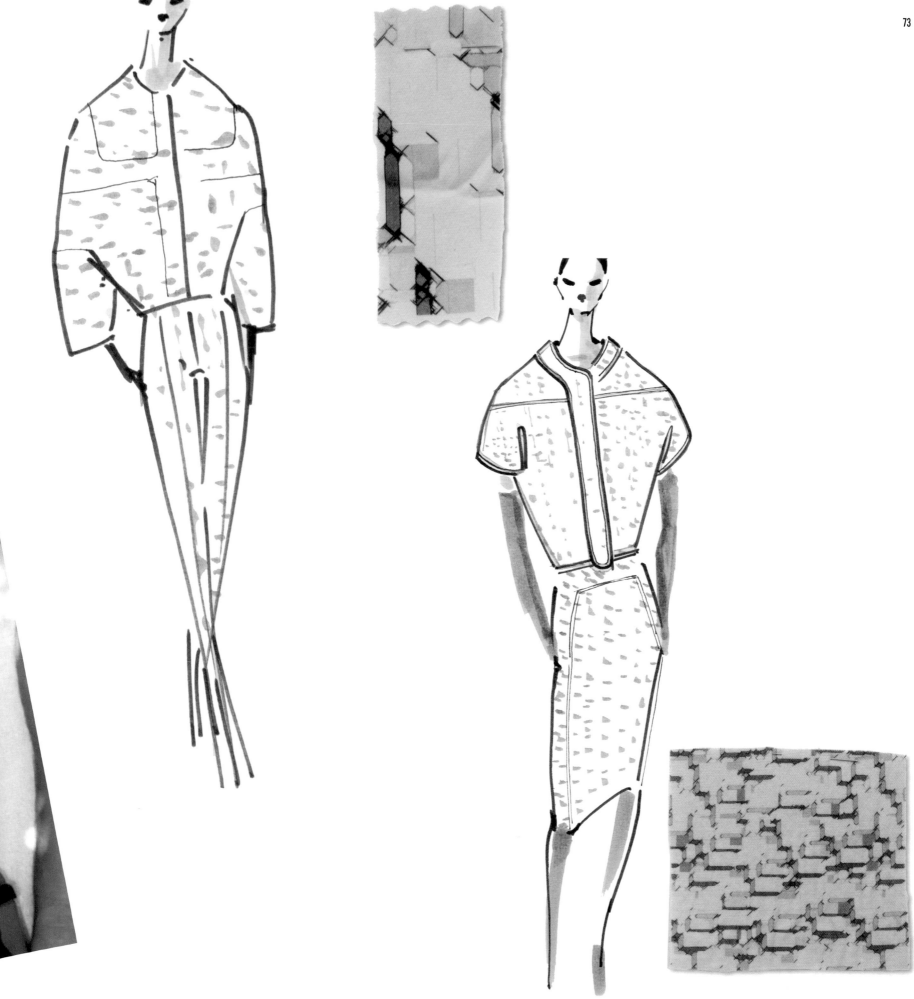

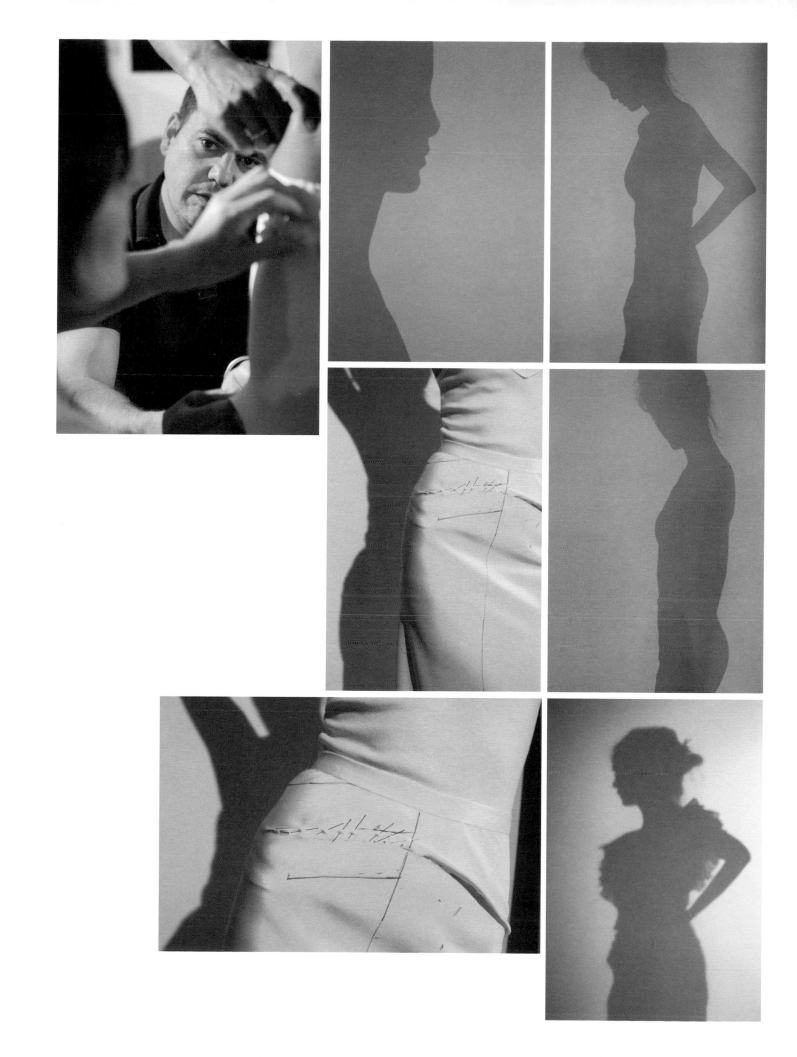

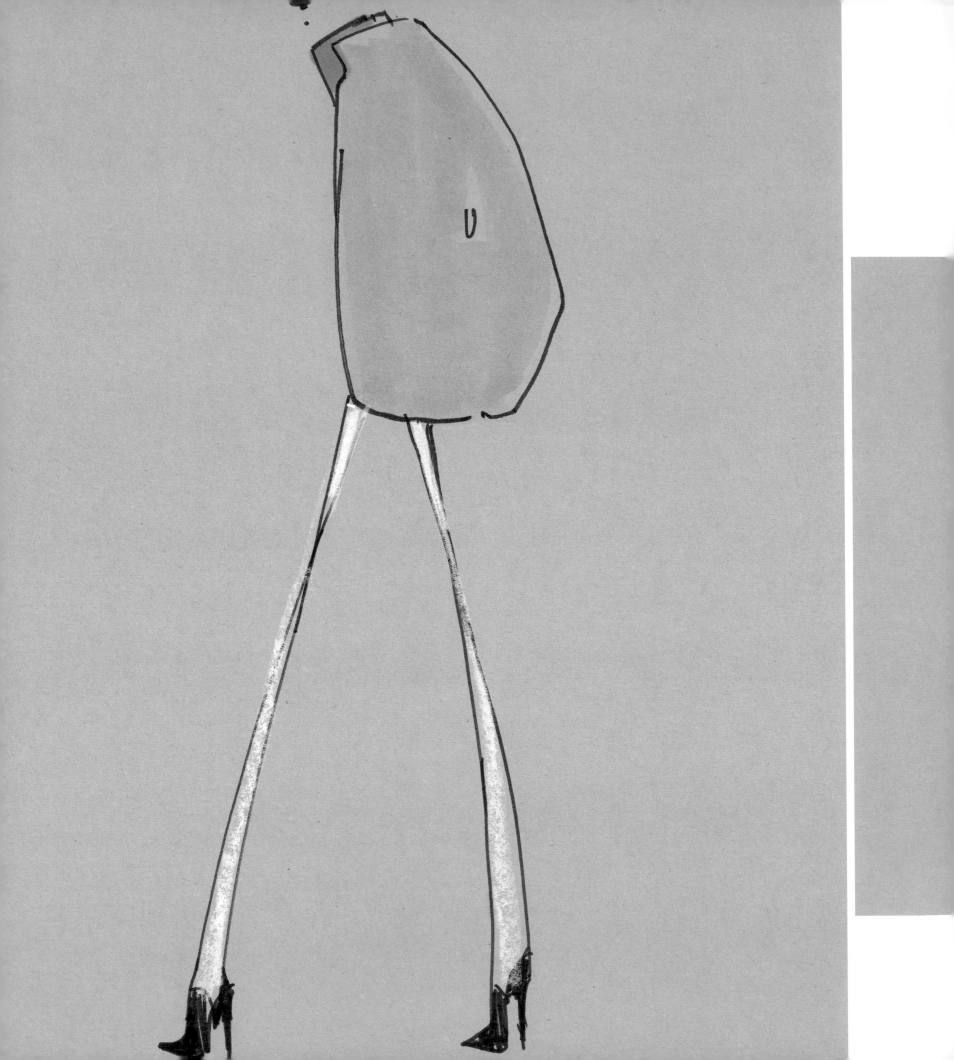

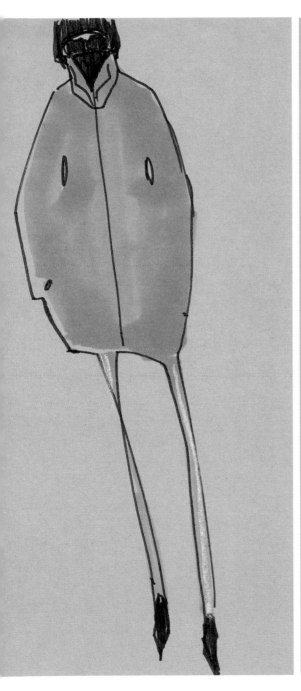
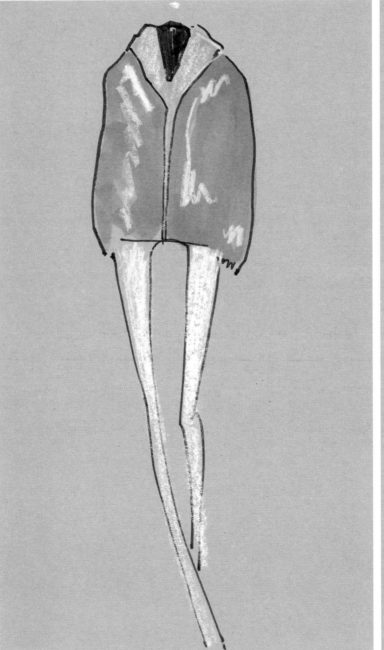
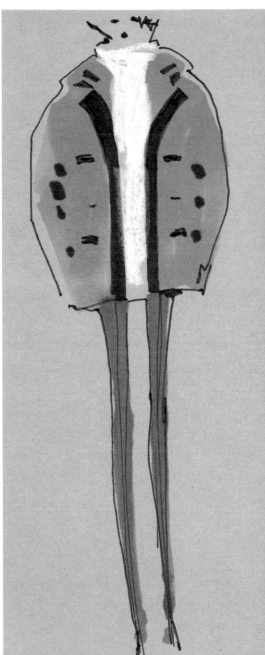

June 27 Rio - beach

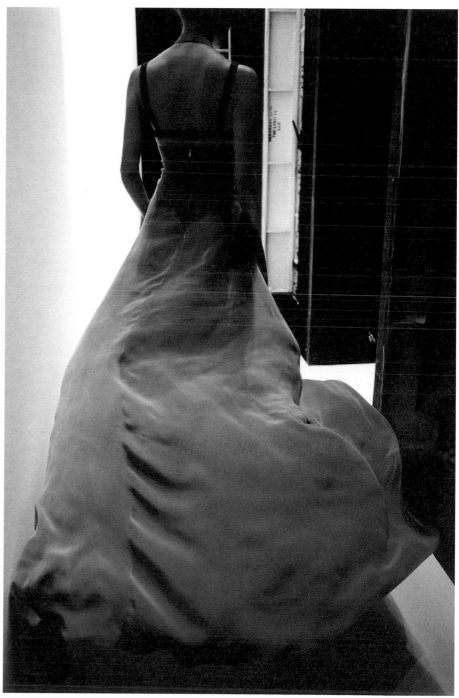

Art, Sex & Wrinkles: A Conversation with Cindy Sherman By Cathy Horyn

Cindy Sherman's sad, hopeful, grotesquely comic women need little interpretation. They are the characters many of us see in our mind's eye, especially those of us who attend a lot of fashion shows in New York or Paris and imagine clothes not merely as a form of theater and self-expression but also as a logical and occasionally horrific extension of personality.

Who would wear that? Well, yes, *who*?

Sherman, while not strictly interested in fashion, uses clothing and makeup for her own purposes—to explore a sexual stereotype, to play with notions of gender and identify, to suggest the dread beyond beauty's surface. She is friends with a number of designers; two years ago, at the urging of a mutual friend, she met Narciso Rodriguez and has since attended his fashion shows. Their meeting was, in a sense, fortuitous. Like Sherman, Rodriguez is guided by a strong aesthetic vision. In their cut and minimal use of decoration, his clothes display a rare economy, an economy of elegance that comes from experience and a preciseness of thinking, which feels modern. Both artist and designer are interested

in each other's world, they see parallels in the treatment of the body, but they remain skeptical of what one art dealer recently called "the visual cultural industry," with mergers between art and the fashion and entertainment industries. Hard judgments, along with certain healthy inhibitions, serve both Sherman and Rodriguez extremely well.

CATHY HORYN: Before you met Narciso, how much did you know about his work?

CINDY SHERMAN: Just enough to think that his clothes were very formfitting. And not being someone who likes curvy, sexy clothes— just because I'm self-conscious—I would go to stores and think, "Oh, gosh, I don't know if I can get away with wearing that."

Cathy Horyn: Surprising as it may sound, not many people realize that Narciso actually does the fittings for his clothes himself. He has that standard in common with Azzedine Alaia in Paris. Watching the process can be eye-opening.

CINDY: I actually did go visit him recently and he said to bring in the things that needed a little adjustment. Which was so interesting. I was kind of afraid to do it, because I didn't want to impose on him or take up his time. But it was fascinating to be on that end—with him feeling the way the fabric goes. There was a skirt with darts in it and

there was some little fold that he couldn't get rid of. He said, "That's why I hate darts—make it a seam." It sort of opened something up to me about his designs. I realized it's all this construction of these pieces, rather than taking one piece and putting darts in it. I'm beginning to understand his sensibility.

CATHY: It's curious how the fashion world is attracted to the extreme, the surreal, the fantastical, rather than anything that's rational, intimate and actual. On my blog at the *Times*, people definitely prefer the latter type of designer—a Narciso, a Raf Simons, an Alber Elbaz. The other kind of fashion, while entertaining, often seems empty and pretentious.

CINDY: Well, I still feel there's so much I don't know about what goes into designing anything. In that sense, I'm still kind of intimidated by the whole process, like it's some art form I don't really understand. I get a sense that Narciso cares a lot about subtle things. Once you get so big and have so much funding behind you, you relegate so much of the decision-making to teams. Some of that control might get lost. It seems that he is so involved in every stage himself.

CATHY: What do you think, in general, of the scene at fashion shows, the hierarchy of the front row?

CINDY: I definitely observe the other people there. I do feel like I'm an outsider with a very privileged place. And most of those people look familiar to me but I don't know why. It's like viewing another culture under a microscope. Also, I know that they don't know who I am, so they're wondering, "What's she doing in the first row?" I look at the other rows and wonder if they feel resentful of the people sitting in front of them.

CATHY: Probably. How much do you think about clothes or investigate what's new?

CINDY: When I'm actually working I'm not thinking about fashion at all. I think of it as just necessary bits of costume that have to come together to form a character. But I think my work is informed a lot by what I see in fashion, whether it's on the street or in a magazine or store. I love to shop and look at clothes and study them. I was in a store looking at some clothes and the sales clerk—maybe thinking I was one of those people who copy clothes—said to me, "Oh, you're really studying that closely." I felt very self-conscious. Because I wasn't buying anything; I was just looking. I love to imagine how something is worn, or how unwearable it is to me, or how, as an object, it's just so pleasing.

CATHY: But your specific choices of clothing have evoked so much feeling in your images. I was looking recently at your photographs in the eighties—the centerfolds and a series in which you used Gaultier's famous conical corset. All very transgressive at the time.

CINDY: I did some stuff for a store called Diane B, and they were going to be ads in *Artforum*, so I borrowed some clothes. She was great. She said, "Do whatever you want." So I played around and after that, a guy from Dorothée Bis asked me about doing some ads for French *Vogue*. They thought I was just going to re-create what I had done for Diane B, like some kind of amusing pictures. Instead I did these more disturbing pictures of women with bloody noses and scarred faces. French Vogue hated it. But it sort of triggered me into using fake blood and fake noses, and going in a more ugly direction. I did other things in the early nineties for Comme des Garçons. It was really fun and by then people were saying, "Do whatever you want." That was really freeing. Other than that, I don't know how

fashion has influenced me. Up until the early nineties, I don't remember a cultural awareness of labels in fashion. Nowadays, teenagers know Gucci and Prada.

CATHY: Narciso, as you know, just created a partnership with Liz Claiborne. He's been doing some of his best work in recent seasons, despite having very little money. Money can make a big difference. It can liberate you, allow you to move forward. I had the feeling you went through this process in the mid-nineties, when you decided to photograph mannequin parts. Why is this so important for a creative person?

CINDY: It's a scary thing to do. A lot of people just want to repeat what they're known for. They know that everybody still likes it.

CATHY: I remember saying to Narciso a year before the Liz deal, "Just think what you could do with more resources, better fabrics." We've seen the difference with other designers. They become more daring and innovative.

CINDY: I think it's important just to keep the creative spirit fresh. For me, it's important when I work that I don't get bored. I get bored really easily with what I do. As soon as I feel like I'm repeating myself, I try to move on. At the core of my work, there are still a lot of the same elements—using myself, the idea of portraiture—but I get scared of falling into a routine and just doing that over and over again.

CATHY: Does an involvement with the fashion world somehow hurt or undermine an artist?

CINDY: Oh, I don't think so. Well, I don't know. Maybe hanging out too much in the fashion world and not making your art, I suppose. Spending too much money on clothes. I think it's interesting when art uses fashion.

CATHY: I just read a fascinating profile of Jeffrey Deitch in the *New Yorker*. He said the art world used to be a community, but now it's an industry—"a visual cultural industry," like the film and fashion industries, and he pointed to the various crossovers.

CINDY: It's sad but true. And I don't think the art world should be like that. I don't think artists should be considered celebrities.

CATHY: When you finish a series of photographs, and you come out of character and costume, do you feel exhausted?

CINDY: I usually have a hard time doing anything social. I just feel so wrapped up in my head that it's hard to go out and talk about movies or what's happening in life. I'm not used to talking! If things are going well when I'm working, I feel energized by the process. Usually I'm having fun, so it's not like some deep emotional thing.

CATHY: Do you ever laugh at your transformations?

CINDY: Oh, yeah.

CATHY: Do you own a status handbag?

CINDY: Yeah, too many [*laughs*]. I mean, I don't really know what this season's It bag is. I remember the season of the Prada bowling ball bag, like the black-and-white one. I got it early on, but it just seemed a status bag that I was afraid to use. So, finally, after seeing it reproduced in magazines, I thought, "I guess I had better use it now." I used it two or three days and then I thought, "It's over! It's already in the magazines!" I think I sold it on eBay.

CATHY: The subject of sex and fashion really fascinates me, partly because we went through a period after Gaultier in the eighties in which nothing shocked us. Of course, designers like Narciso and Alaia have always done sexy clothes in a contemporary way. Tom Ford attempted to push things further. Now, apparently the most popular Halloween costumes for girls are from *Playboy*, sexy cheerleading and cocktail outfits. These are notions that people objected to—and misunderstood—when you were doing your centerfold series, work that you took quite seriously.

CINDY: Maybe it's just a phase our culture is going through. When I was going trick-or-treating, I was always a monster or an old lady. But my girlfriends—I remember thinking, "Why do they have to be brides or ballerinas?" They were always trying to be pretty. Now, in addition to being pretty, girls want to be sexy. I'm sure that it has something to do with our culture. I can't imagine where it's going from here. It obviously has to do with an insecurity that young women still feel, the need to be paid attention to for looking pretty.

CATHY: I'm sure that most women don't have an argument with wanting to look pretty. Still, I wince when I hear a designer say, "I just want to make women look beautiful." Talk about being turned into stone.

CINDY: I've explored a lot of stuff that's the opposite of traditional beauty. For me, when I get dressed, I want to look good but I also want to look interesting—more than beautiful. In this country, so many people obsess over fashion, and in this city, they feel they have to look perfect. With manicures and pedicures and your hair blown out. And that's in addition to the perfect outfit and bag. When I was in France recently I was struck by how many women were not doing the whole makeup and manicure thing. They were dressed beautifully but they didn't care about the whole package being groomed and perfect.

CATHY: I don't know, at this stage of my life, I kind of want to go more beautiful than interesting.

CINDY: [*With a laugh*] Now that you say that, as I get older I don't mind going backwards in certain ways. What used to bother me politically—now I don't really care. You're making amends because you've got wrinkles.

CATHY: Amen to that.

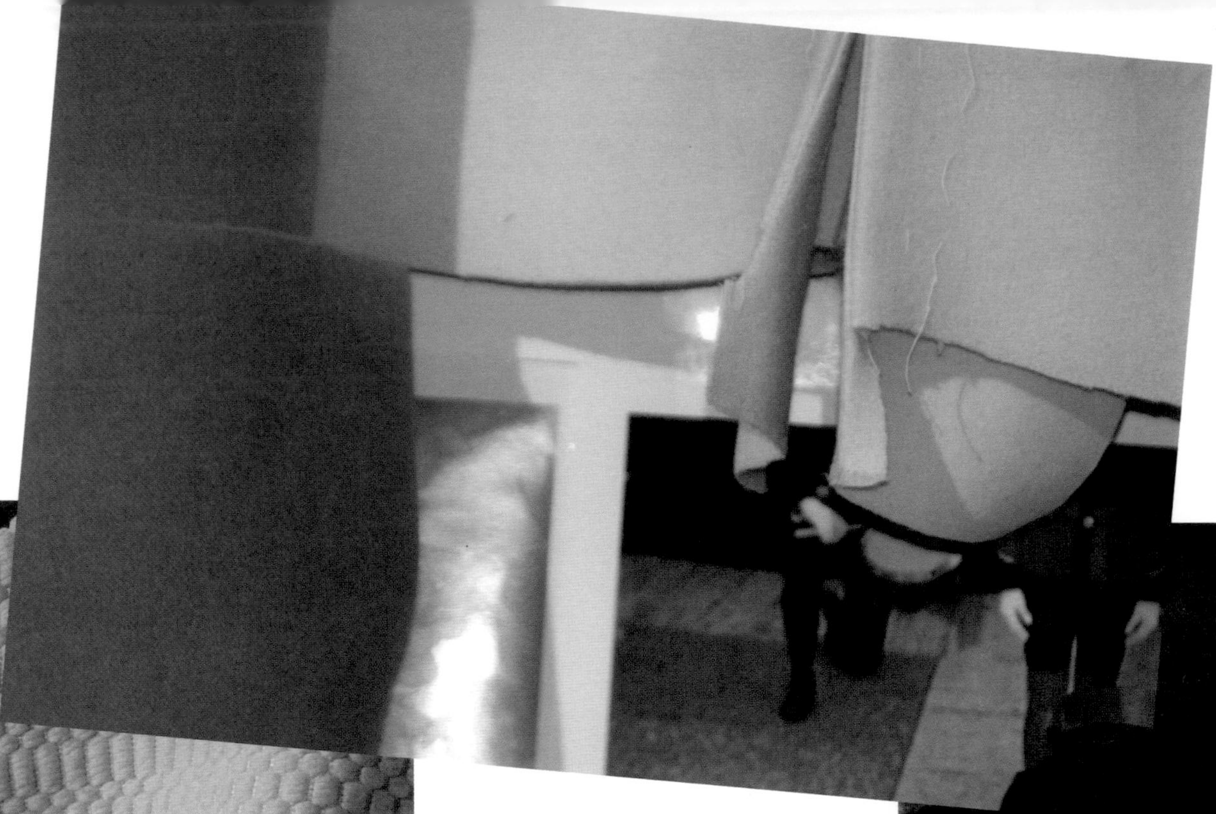

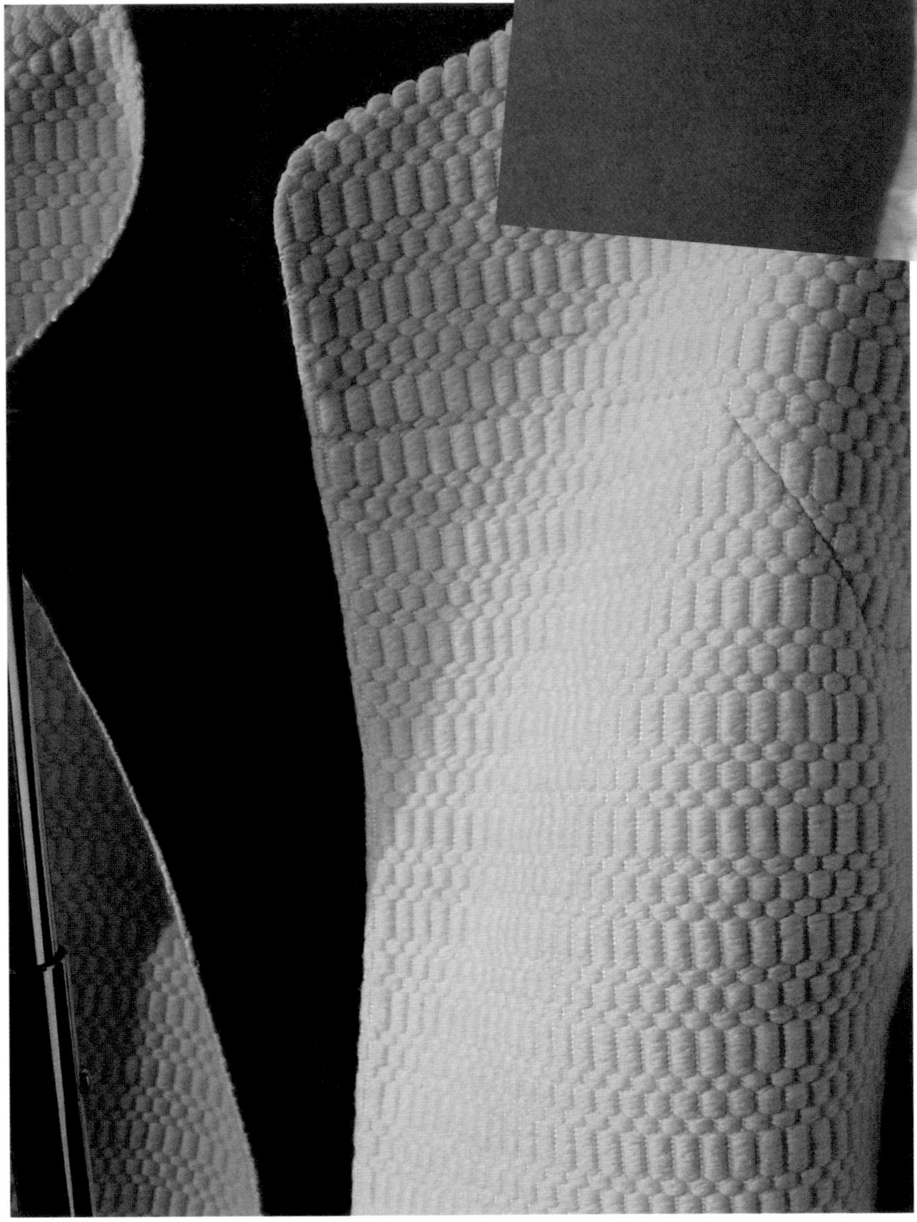

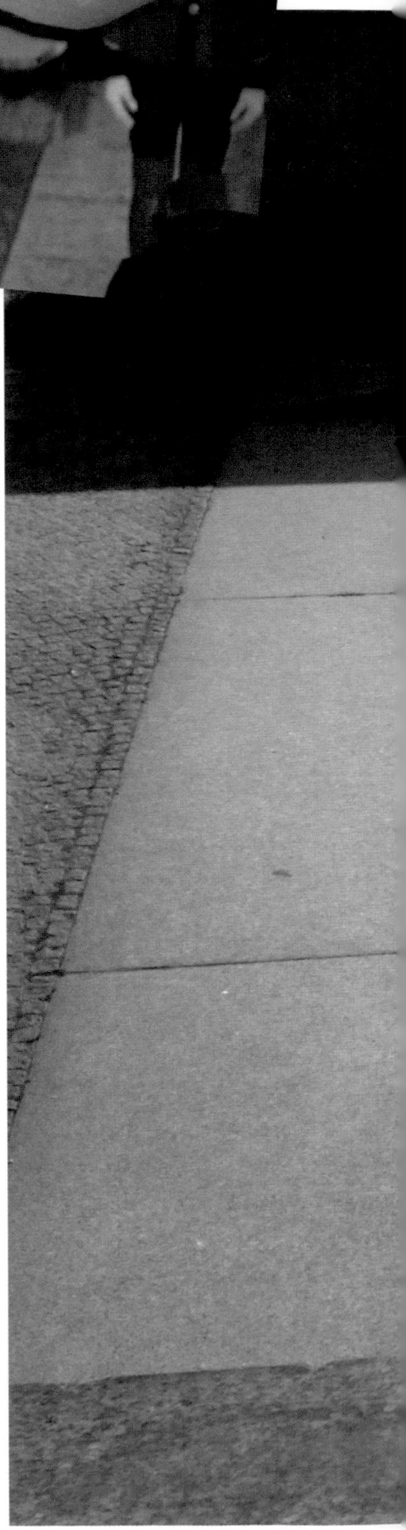

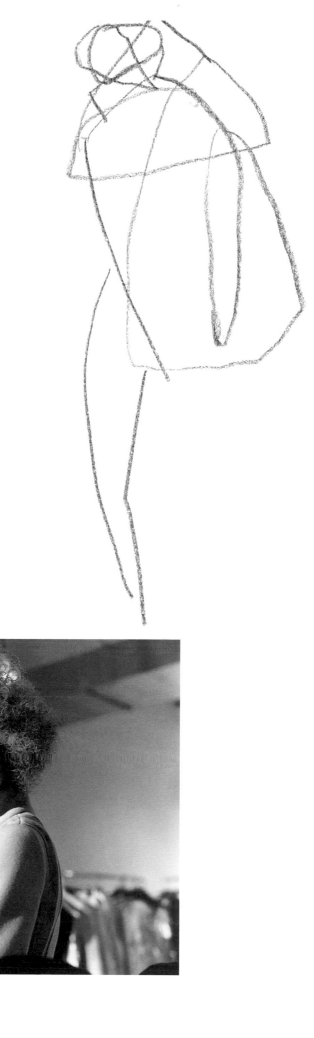

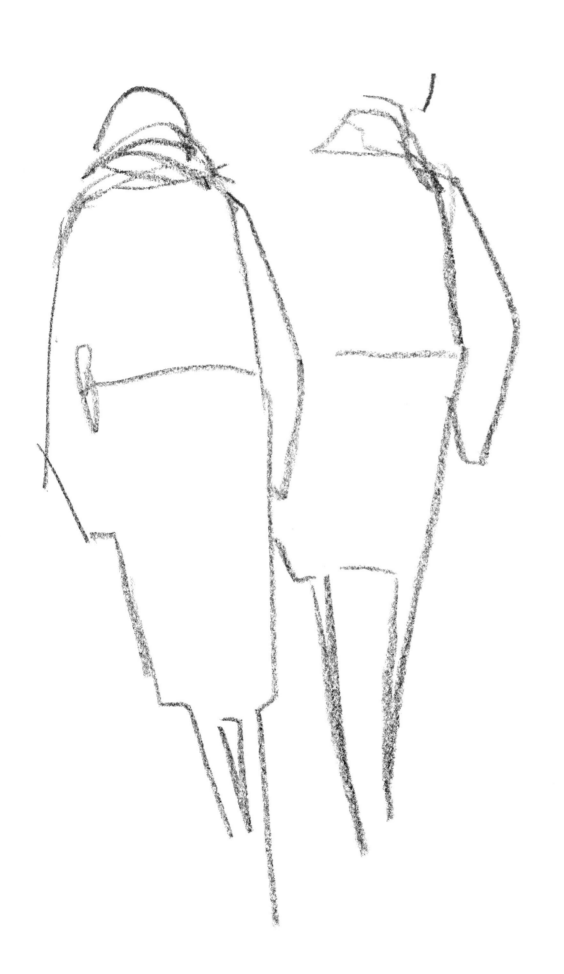

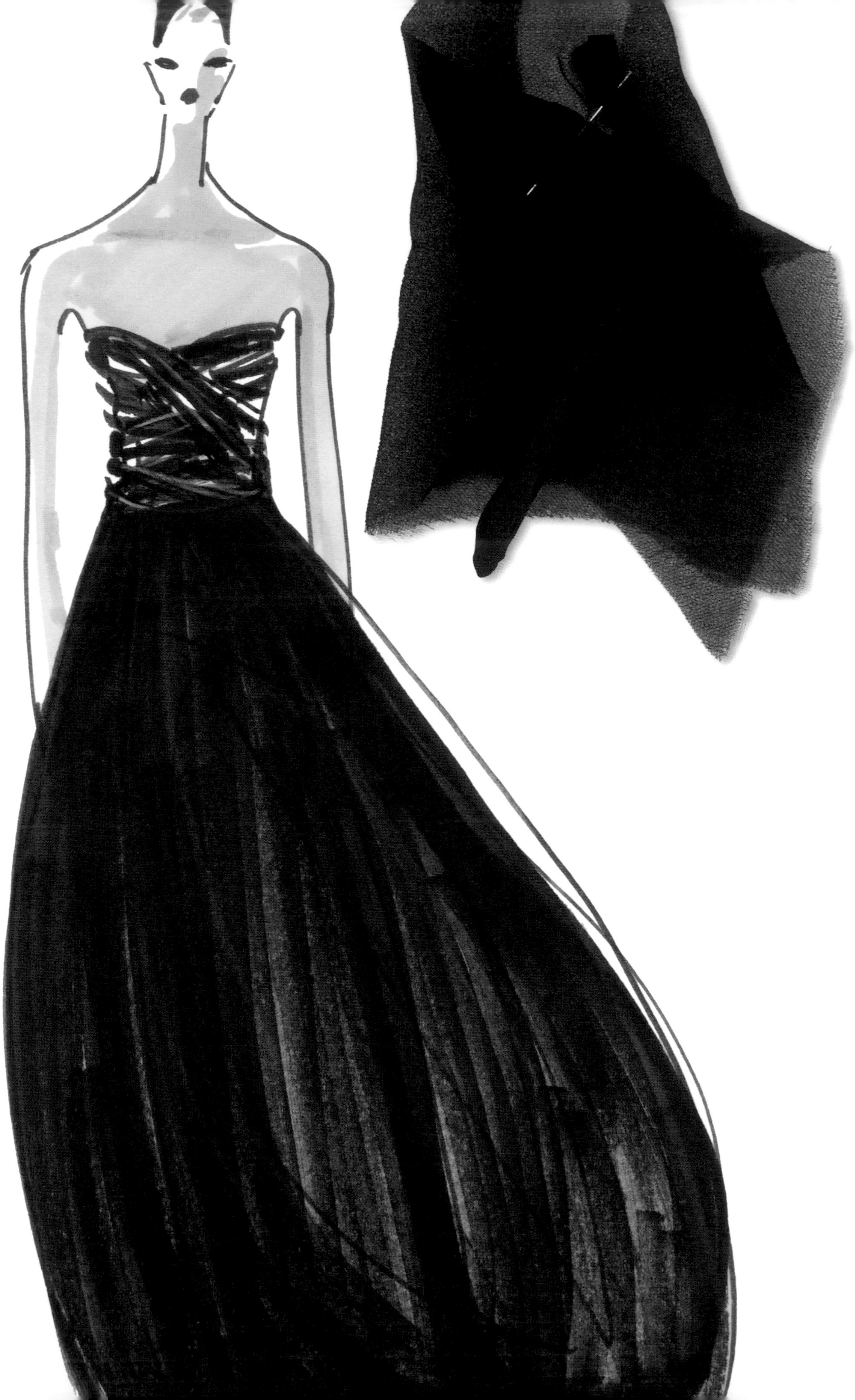

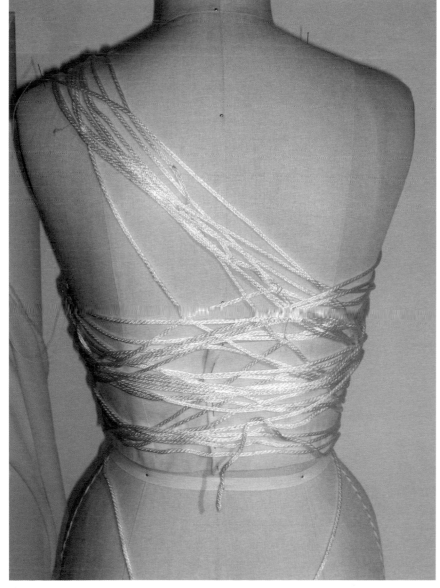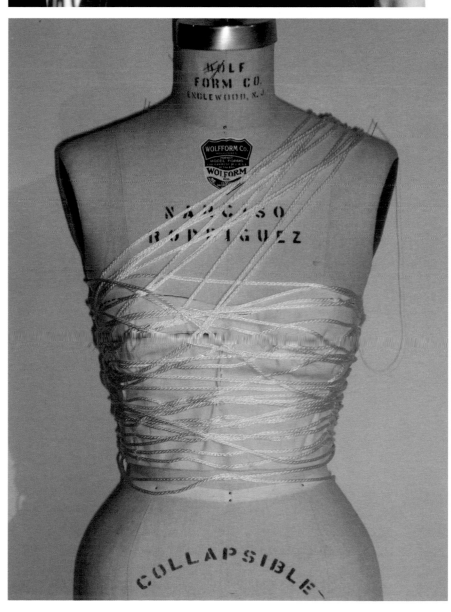

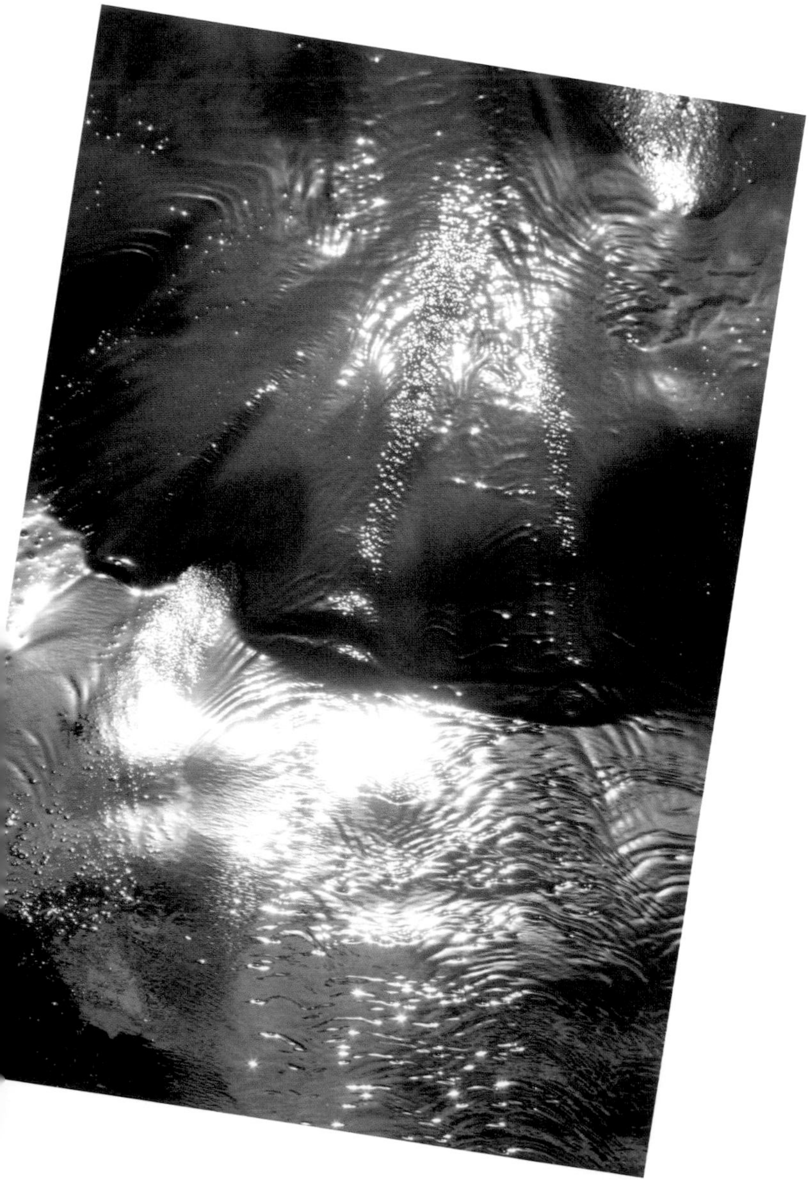

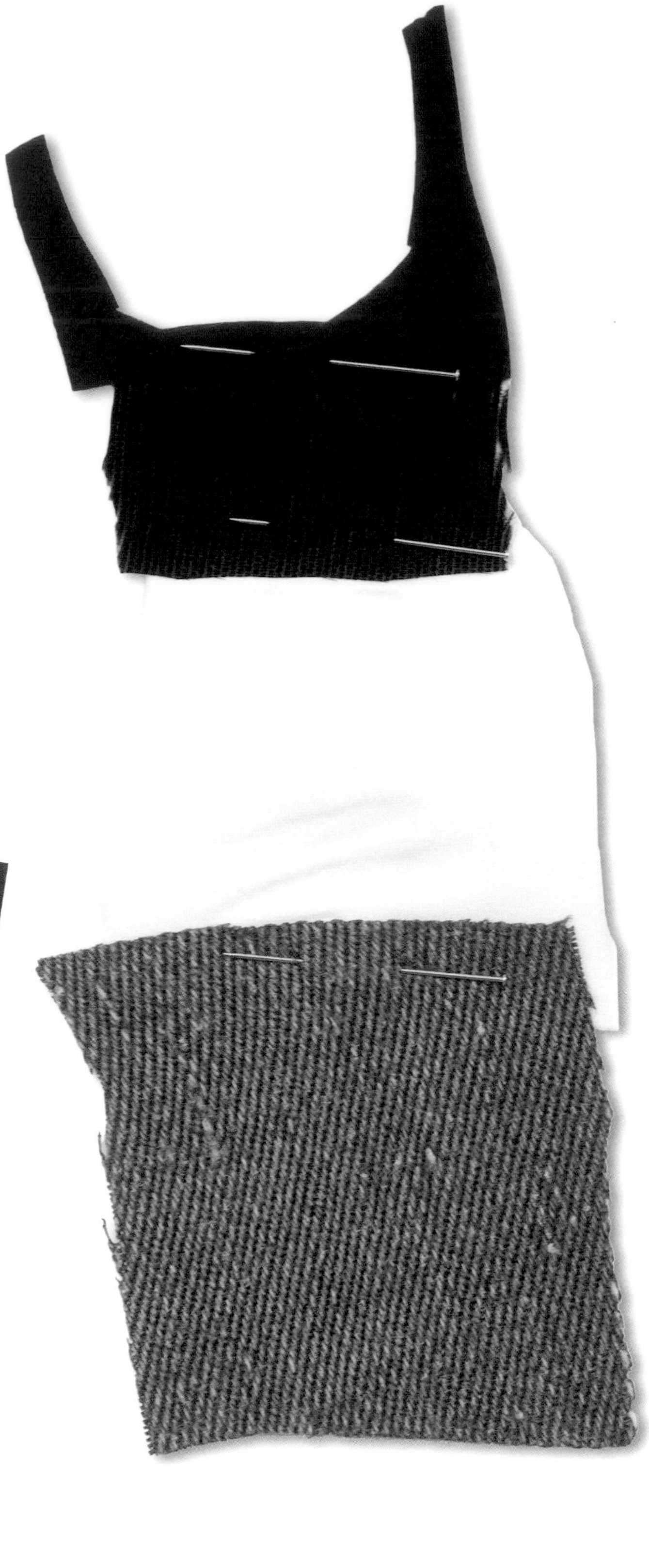

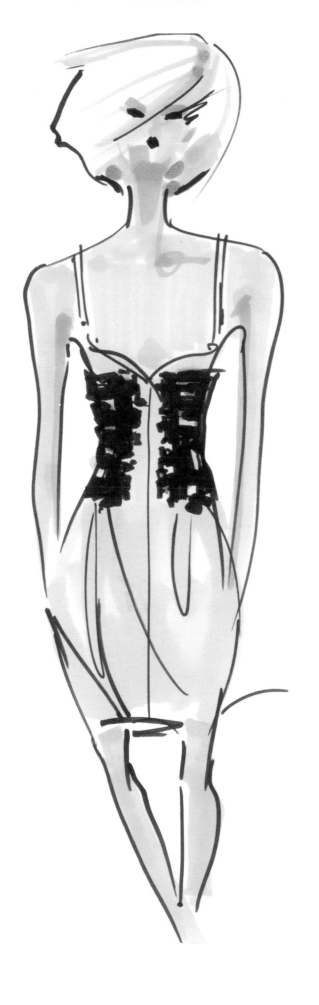

Rio
2007

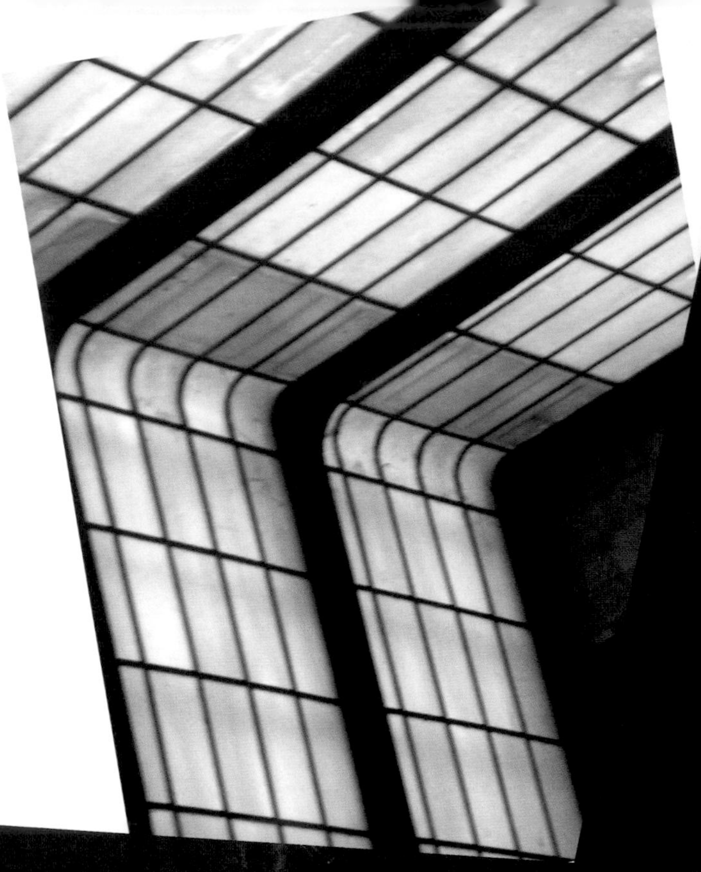

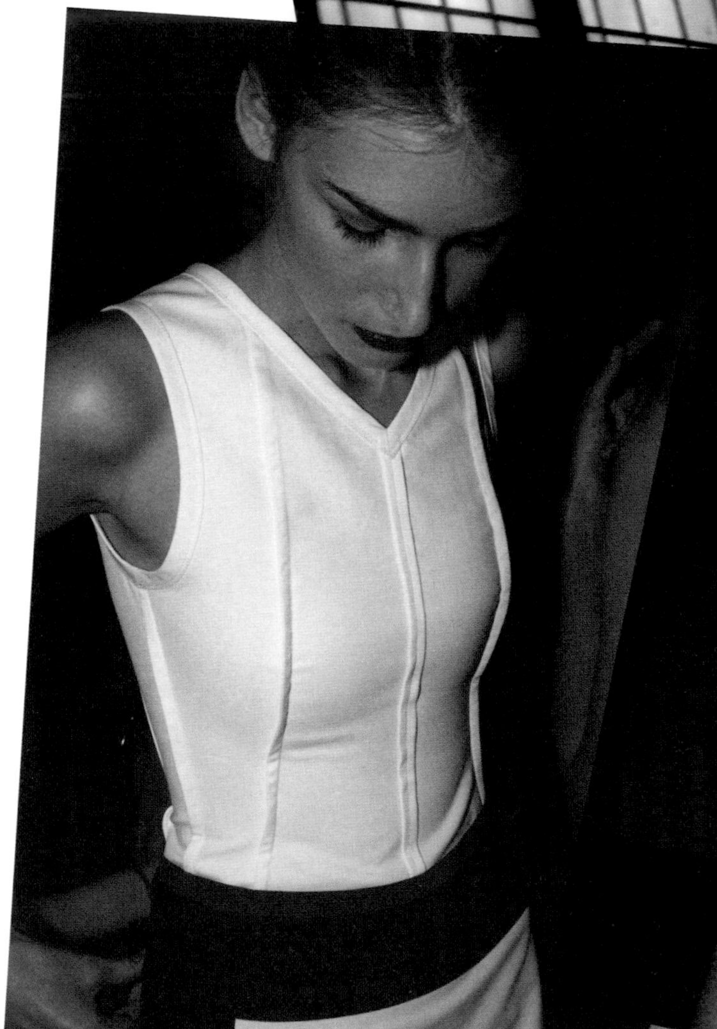

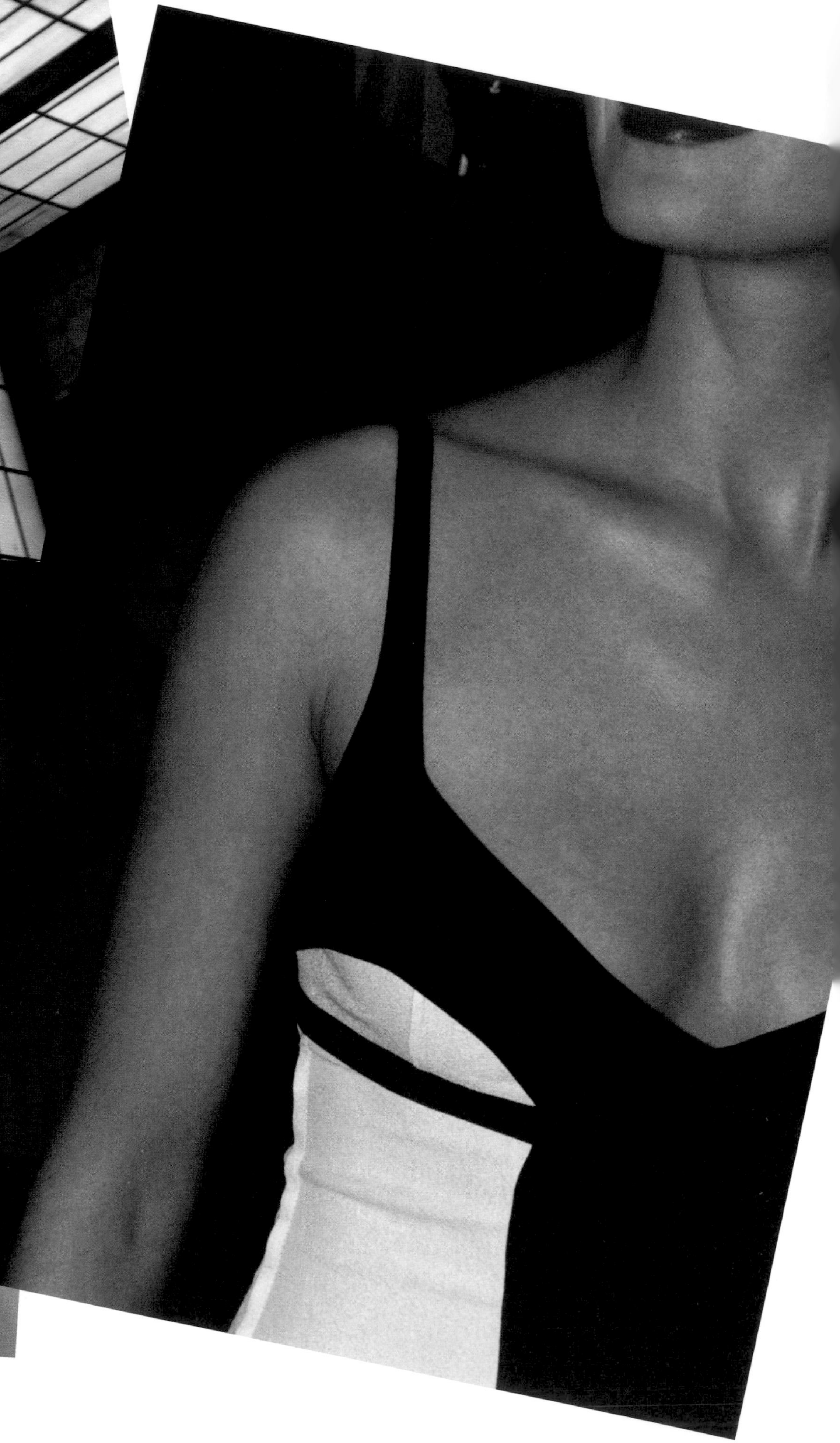

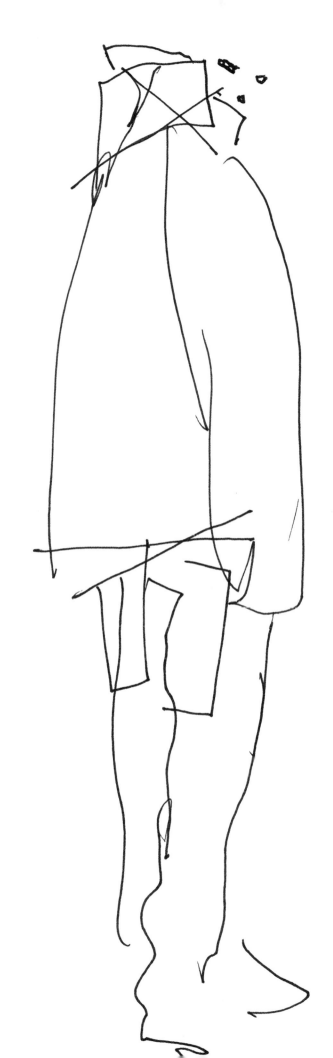

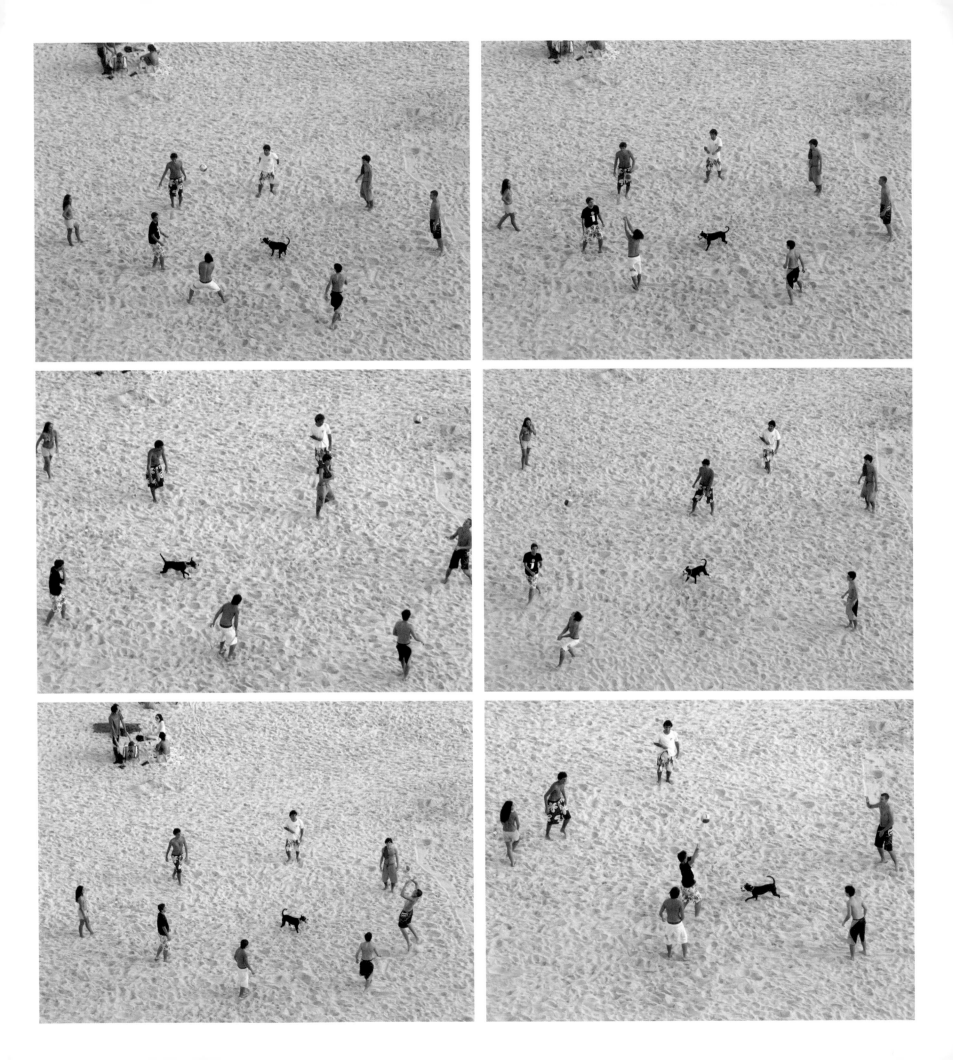

Caetano Veloso and Narciso Rodriguez

NARCISO RODRIGUEZ: Caetano, you are Brazil…

CAETANO VELOSO: Thank you.

NARCISO: … and such an inspiration to me—you and Brazil. I want to speak to you about Rio and everything that inspires me about this country. I am fascinated by the wave of graffiti that envelops Rio and São Paulo today, and also the art of Hélio Oiticica. On a trip to London I saw a spectacular exhibit of his work and your photos at the Tate Modern. I bought some books then, and have gotten others since. It is my biggest influence at the moment—that period of rebirth, in the sixties, that you were such an integral part of. It is inspiring to me in so many ways—the youth movement, and how culture took over in Brazil, and how you and Oiticica's work reflected all of that. It's everything that I love about Brazil, the body, the color, and the music all tell me a story. You're such a great storyteller—could you tell me a story from that time?

CAETANO: In 1967, I wrote a song about Brazil. It was filled with violent images, and although they were not precisely descriptive, they were suggestive of many aspects of the country. As you know, we were under military dictatorship at the time, so the lyrics were at once funny and bitter, and somewhat violent. It seemed to me that this was the song that was going to be the center of everything I wanted to do then. The songs I recorded during that time came to comprise the first album of the so-called Tropicalismo movement.

At a party in São Paulo, I saw Luiz Carlos Barreto [a cinematographer of the cinema novo movement, who then went on to become a prominent film producer]. He asked me what I was doing, and I told him about the new album I had recorded. He was crazy about a song I mentioned, inspired by *Terra em transe* [Glauber Rocha's film, for which he was the cinematographer]. So he said to me, "You know, this song sounds like the work of a young artist in Rio called Hélio Oiticica. He has a work called "Tropicália," and you should name this song "Tropicália."

I said I wouldn't give my song the title of somebody else's work, but he insisted that if I saw the work, I would do it. The producer of the record liked the word *Tropicália*, as did my manager, but I told them I didn't want to use anybody else's title in my work. In the meantime, as I was recording other songs, we kept the tapes of that song with "Tropicália" as a provisional title, until we became accustomed to it as the song's final name.

I came to Rio, and a journalist invited me to her house to meet Hélio Oiticica. He knew my work and liked what I had been doing with music. I loved him immediately. He was a completely adorable person—very, very original, spontaneous, highly intelligent, and funny. He was the most sophisticated visual artist in Rio, but you would also find him up in the hills of Mangueira, a favela near Rio, with the guys who danced samba. He knew how to dance like the greatest of Rio's *Pasistas*. He was such an amazing man that I kept the title, and he was very happy that we used it because he liked everything we did. I think this is a beautiful story.

NARCISO: That is an amazing story. I knew your work, but I only recently discovered Oiticica's. It was fascinating for me to see you in his photographs. At the Tate I also saw films of people dancing samba in the Parangolés [wearable works by Oiticica, named after a Brazilian

slang term for a situation of sudden confusion or excitement].

CAETANO: Have you ever seen me wearing a Parangolé?

NARCISO: Yes …

CAETANO: I love that photograph, all those photographs.

NARCISO: It's one of the most beautiful photographs I've ever seen, the color …

CAETANO: … the sky and the colors of the parts of the Parangolé.

NARCISO: That's when I discovered the photograph of you as a fashion model [laughs].

CAETANO: [laughs]

NARCISO: The way that each of those pieces were made was so raw—that is what I love so much about being here in Brazil. Things are very immediate and very natural; even this incredibly thought-out garment was made from painted found objects, things that were also deeply rooted in politics. There was a fantastic one that was an American flag, all white in comparison to all the very colorful pieces that they had put together … it was so inspiring.

The first day I landed here—so many years ago—I met you and Paula, and every time I come back I have another surprise, another gift from this land. It was my dream to come to Rio when I was a kid and I was a fan of yours, so I was lucky to get to know you and love you more than I already did.

CAETANO: I was lucky.

NARCISO: You showed me another part of the country, I fell in love with Rio, and then with Bahia. It was such a huge gift. I always say that when I arrive in Brazil it's another gift placed into my palm.

CAETANO: Yeah, today it's the color of the sky—unbelievable—and the moonrise.

NARCISO: The first place I would own a home is in your country, in Bahia. You took me to Salvador and I learned something else about Brazil. I have always felt connected to Brazil because of our shared African heritage, and my curiosity keeps growing. So even in London my curiosity was drawn back to you, and to Brazil …

CAETANO: Brazil is a funny country. It's the only country in the Americas where Portuguese is spoken, and it's huge, and racially highly mixed.

NARCISO: Yes.

CAETANO: All these things make for a certain responsibility with regard to originality [laughing]—a responsibility to offer an original solution to eternal human problems. Whether we do it or not, we have the opportunity; we are the opportunity.

NARCISO: I've been listening to your music and the music of Brazil since I was a teenager. My first album was of Tania Maria.

CAETANO: Tania is great.

NARCISO: I discovered what the music was and, from there, I learned of you and Gilberto Gil, as well as João Gilberto, Maria Bethânia, and Gal Costa. To discover it personally was amazing, I live in awe of that entire experience.

When you look at this book it would be incomplete if it didn't have those funny pictures of kids surfing, or the girls of Bahia walking down the road, and their beautiful bodies—the nature, the rawness, the sheer sensuality of the people; the work of Niemeyer and the architecture of the hills. It's an important part of my life.

CAETANO: I think Brazil loves having you here.

NARCISO: [laughing together] Thank you, Caetano, that's the greatest compliment.

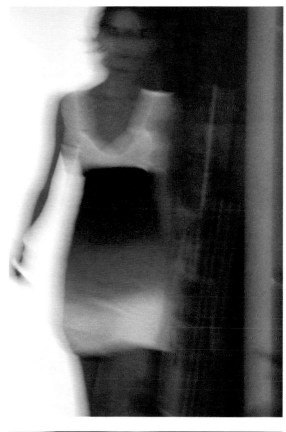

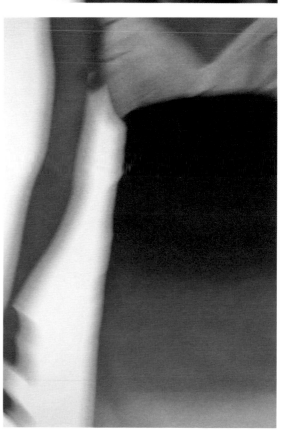

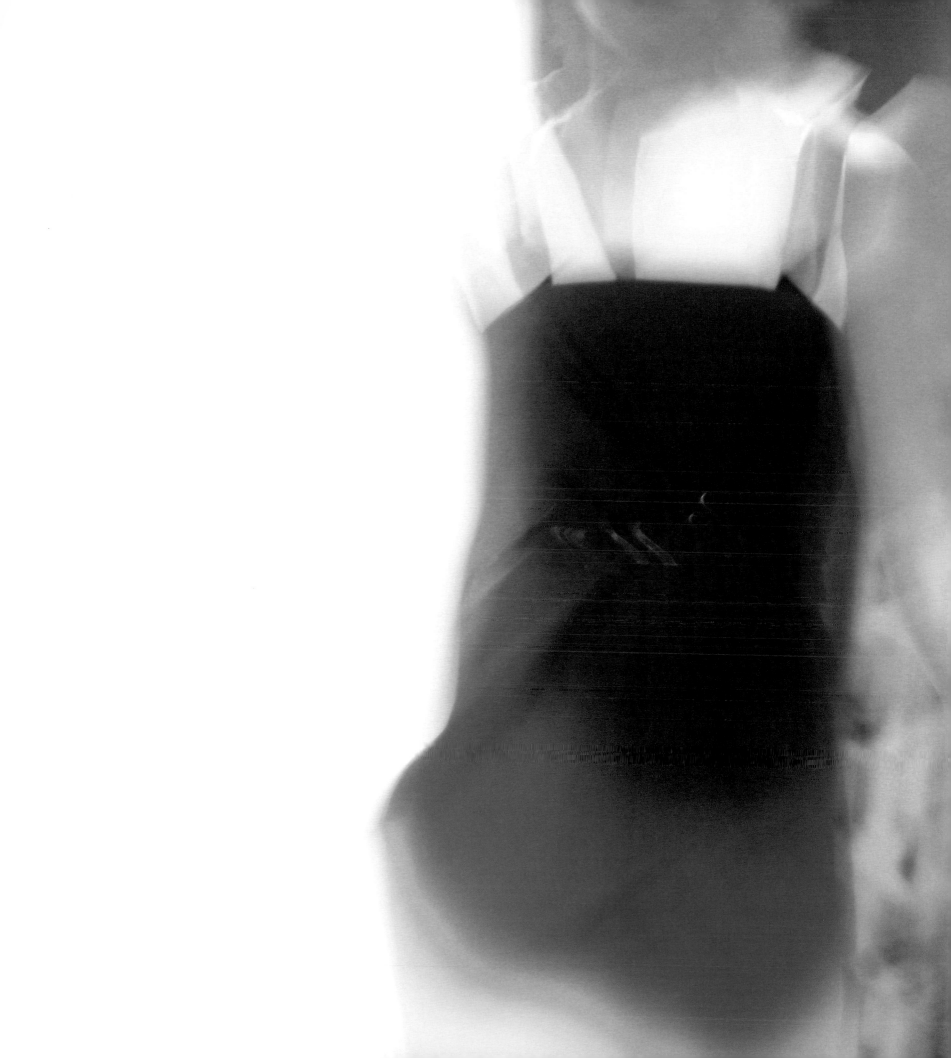

Sean Taylor

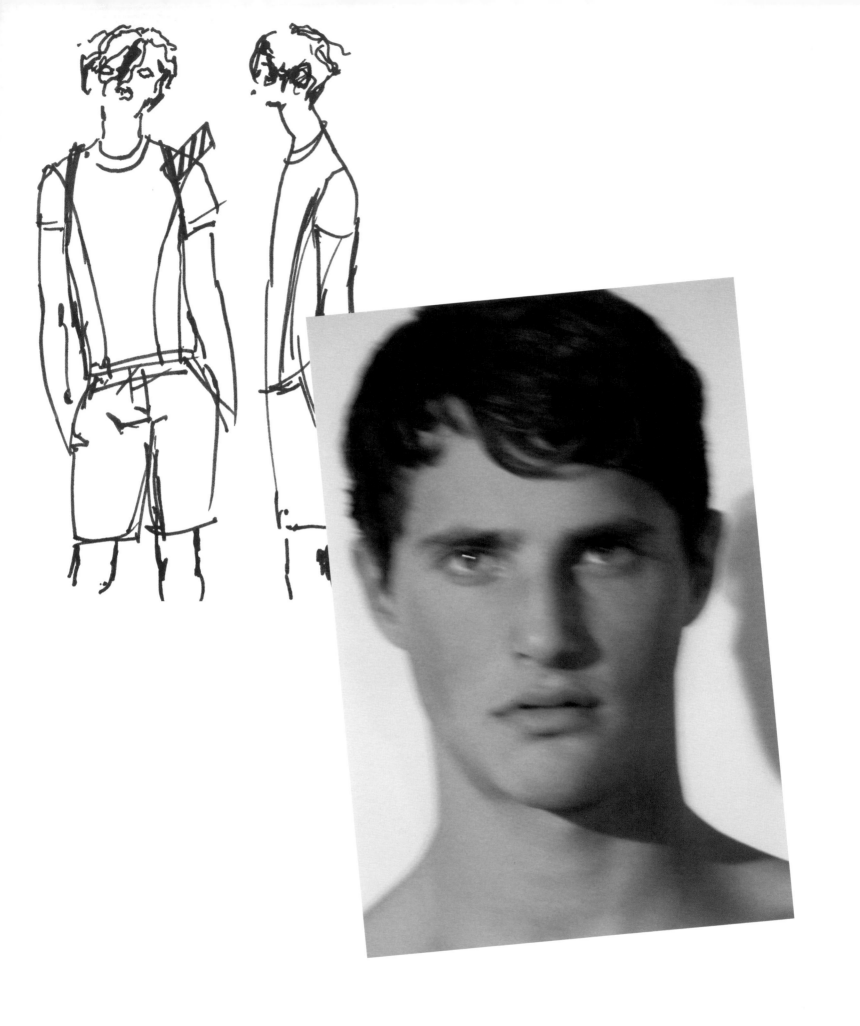

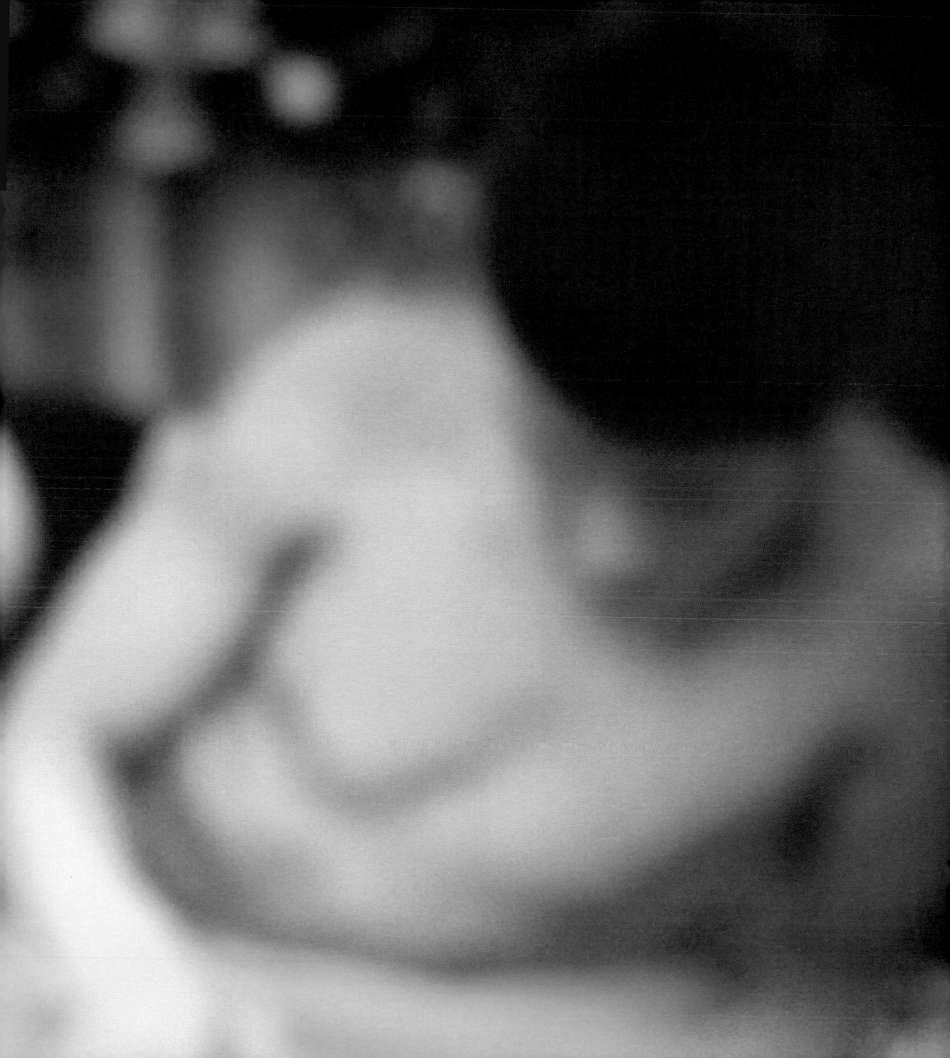

March 30

(73) (48) (73)

15:00   85   140
30:00   2.05 092
12:00   .60   115
_____
57:00   3.50 515

Astor Place Morning traffic

Rachel Weisz and Narciso Rodriguez

RACHEL: I met you because of a red dress that I wore to a premiere in L.A. It was a knee-length, fitted red dress with two spaghetti straps that fastened behind my neck.

NARCISO: The famous red dress…

RACHEL: It was the most extraordinary feeling to be inside that dress. I've never felt more like myself, like I could just go in and handle that red carpet because I was wearing the most perfect dress. And I remember I also wore a pair of pointy black shoes of yours. I felt sexy and strong. I just remember thinking, *wow!*—and I hadn't even met you. When we finally met I saw your beautiful face and your sweetness and intelligence and curiosity about the world and other

people. I had imagined I was going to meet a really scary, bitchy diva. [*laughs*] It's a very organic thing, the way you work, the way you design and collaborate with women. I think it's pretty unusual in the fashion world.

NARCISO: I'm very lucky that I get to create for women who inspire me.

RACHEL: Right, and at special moments in their lives, like when I was pregnant and nominated for an Oscar, you made my dress.

NARCISO: It was such an exciting time.

RACHEL: That was unbelievable. You showed me the embroideries on the black dress, and on the white dress. And you even came with me to the ceremony—you were my date along with my boyfriend. You also made an incredible maternity dress for Sarah Jessica Parker when she was pregnant. And I know she tells everyone that it was one of her favorite dresses ever. All the dresses that I've ever worn from you have been iconic—for example, the green one for the premiere of *The Constant Gardener.*

NARCISO: You looked so beautiful that night.

RACHEL: Remember the time I was here and I had on the green dress—the one that was in American *Vogue* with the belt on it? And you were looking and thinking, "Mm-m, it just needs something…" Then you pulled out a black sash and tied it, kimono style…

NARCISO: Right.

RACHEL: …suddenly it became something else that's just right. I really admire that about you—how you can take one relatively small detail and transform the entire look. Your dresses—even your T-shirts are sexy. It makes me think, "*Ahh*…you must be a woman because

I love this dress, and it loves me." [*laughs*] You understand what worries me, what makes me anxious, and what is going to make me feel good. When I met you, it confirmed my suspicion that you were a man who genuinely loved women. I could tell that you're not afraid of their power, their complexity, and their mischievousness. You just get it and embrace it all. And that's unusual, I think.

NARCISO: I love to work on special things for special people, like when Carolyn [Bessette-Kennedy] asked me to make her wedding dress. She was someone I loved very much and the dress needed to be a perfect frame for her personality and her beauty.

RACHEL: Over the years I've seen many women come up to you and say, "Oh, I love wearing your dresses because…" And I always see how fulfilled you get from meeting these real women who are wearing

your dresses, and hearing how they feel in them. Then when I come up to your studio and you've got a collection brewing—which is all the time, of course—I see the intellectual side of your process in your inspiration boards around the studio: photographs you've taken of people who intrigue you, pictures of people on the street, images of Brancusi sculptures, close-ups of American football players. So how do you create a mood for the concept of a collection?

NARCISO: Today it's *Alien 3*. Tomorrow, who knows? I am constantly taking pictures of life on the street and on the beach: what people are wearing—or what they're not wearing—and their spirit, their bodies. It could be things that have nothing to do with fashion, like people rushing to work. It's much more emotional for me that way—to look at someone and imagine what's inside. Or if they have something specific on, I think, "Why would they choose to wear that?"

RACHEL: I understand.

NARCISO: I like to see how people present themselves to the world, who they are, the way they move. Like the man who's been wearing the same suit since 1979—it's been so perfectly laundered for so many years that it's taken on the shape of his body instead of what it used to be.

RACHEL: In that sentence, you told a story. Your eye is like a novelist's eye. It was very poetic when you said that the humanist in you is drawn to the story of this man through his clothes: how he kept this suit so carefully for all these years, and how amazing it is that it has changed to fit his body. It's like you're a detective reading the clothes. You read them the way you would read a poem. In a way, your clothes do what that man's suit did when it took on the shape of his body. They hug the body until they're like your skin. When I have on one of your dresses I barely notice that I've got it on. It's engineered so well that once it's on the person, it just stays on and you don't have to worry about anything. It molds to the shape of your skin; it's like the cliché that you should wear the dress, the dress shouldn't wear you. I think that shows humility on your part. You say you don't want the noise, so there's a quietness. It's clear that a very high level of engineering and conceptual design has gone into the dress. Talking about your process, you've said you're reconstructing clothes…

NARCISO: I'm interested in *seeing* the work that goes into the process. It slowly evolves from the way you fit a garment to how you construct it and expose that construction so that the beauty is the detail. I'm interested in seeing the body and the way the seams lay over one another, or how extra stitching supports the bust more or less in certain places. It becomes more of a play on exposing and revealing the process.

RACHEL: [*laughs*] You're saying that you do expose the process instead of hiding it? What's normally on the inside is on the outside?

NARCISO: I like the idea of duality and mystery: what you see on the outside and what you are on the inside. That was the inspiration for the fragrance and the concept for the bottle. There is this beautiful, pure object, but you're really not quite sure what's on the inside; you have to experience it, fall in love with it. Those abstract romantic inspirations are always a part of my work: the way things are much more detailed on the back, or, conversely, they're completely backless. I think it's beautiful when a woman walks into a room and peoples' heads turn to follow her.

RACHEL: Like in the song "The Girl from Ipanema," she passes by and everybody says, "*Ahh!*"

Christopher Wheeldon and Narciso Rodriguez
Moderated by Betsy Berne

NARCISO RODRIGUEZ: When you were looking for a collaborator on your next project, why did you decide to call me—was it random?

CHRISTOPHER WHEELDON: It wasn't random; no, it was not random by any means. We wanted to create a collaboration between different art forms, crossing over between popular culture and fashion. So it wasn't just about having costumes designed by a costume designer. We started to think about who is supposed to be the light from the fire. And we thought, "Narciso would be fantastic, because his clothes are always so classic, but they're classic interpretations of something very current." It seemed like a perfect mix, the perfect match with us. So we came and we sat at this table. We said, "Will you design the scenes for our first creation as a company?" And he didn't even hesitate. He said, "Absolutely." But not only did he say "Absolutely," he also said, "I want to design the costumes for all of the ballets," which was fantastic and incredibly generous, but we couldn't do that, because a lot of them had already been designed. So that's really how it began.

NARCISO: Chris took me to see *Nightingale and the Rose*.

CHRISTOPHER: *Nightingale and the Rose* is a ballet I created last spring as resident choreographer for the New York City Ballet. I thought that before we started working on this new piece, I should take Narciso to see something that I had done. And we listened to the music for the new ballet.

NARCISO: It was a beautiful day. We listened to the most amazing music. He gave me a silent film to watch.

CHRISTOPHER: It's called *The Dying Swan*. It's actually the music that ended up becoming a score for *Fool's Paradise*, which had been written originally as a trio for a soundtrack, a contemporary soundtrack, to another silent movie from the nineteen-thirties. *The Dying Swan* is an old Russian silent movie about a ballerina. I gave Narciso the silent movie with the soundtrack on. We listened to the music. We sketched a little.

NARCISO: It was one of those serendipitous moments. Every time he comes in, it's like that. The ballet was gorgeous. I was so moved when I saw it, it just felt so different. And then came the rehearsal …

CHRISTOPHER: … at the Duke Studios, on 42nd Street. That must have been July. I had completed the Prokofiev pas de deux, and Narciso came to watch it.

NARCISO: It was the second time that I was so deeply moved by seeing Chris's work. I'd had a stressful, packed day, and I had to be somewhere at two o'clock for a meeting that had been rescheduled many times. And I just stopped, ran uptown to 42nd Street, and walked in. I only had fifteen minutes.

CHRISTOPHER: You stayed for two hours.

NARCISO: We stayed for two hours.

CHRISTOPHER: You cancelled your meeting.

NARCISO: We cancelled everything. I grabbed Chris, the two dancers, and dragged everyone downtown to my office.

CHRISTOPHER: And you tried some prototypes. We were eating lunch, and there were ladies in the back busily interpreting what Narciso wanted. And then suddenly, by the end of lunch, something came out. And we put it on the dancers and started to talk. I remember you saying, "We want to see the shape of the movement, the shape of the bodies interacting."

NARCISO: I was very aware of what they needed to wear, but also very aware of how Chris's work is about the body. And about sexuality—but in a very graceful way. I loved when Maria appeared en pointe.

CHRISTOPHER: Yes, it's very unusual, the way she slides along en pointe.

NARCISO: Unbelievable.

CHRISTOPHER: Well, one thing that I love to do is to explore the use of the pointe shoe, and how it can be used in a way that's unconventional. It's sort of fun.

NARCISO: We either have to create something that's traditional—working in the vein of what's traditional—or be avant-garde. And It's much harder to do what Chris does, or what I do, which is to provoke, but not provoke to turn people away. Our aim is to bring more people in, make it more approachable.

CHRISTOPHER: I think it's about broad appeal, because you know that if you go so bizarrely way out with something, you're actually going to turn people off. Yet if you take something that already has resonance for a certain generation of people, and then find a way to make that appeal to their grandchildren, then what you're doing is creating something that encompasses everyone. And I think that's what the theater is about, because everyone's going to want to buy tickets.

BETSY BERNE: So it was an intense collaboration.

CHRISTOPHER: The design for the costumes pretty much came from our conversation. And from having seen *Nightingale and the Rose*, but never actually seeing *Fool's Paradise*. He knew what it was that he thought might work, and I know the work as we were conversing, I had it in my head. So I could tell that our ideas were meshing beautifully.

BETSY: Is there a theatrical element to your clothes?

CHRISTOPHER: I think there is a theatrical element to Narciso's clothes, but it's not overtly theatrical. It's poetic. There is a kind of magical eroticism there, without being in any way overtly sexual. The costumes were a direct extension of the bodies, the movement, and the music.

BETSY: Like a second skin?

NARCISO: It was really …

BETSY: … all about nudity.

NARCISO: It was not about nudity in the sense that anything was pornographic, or vulgar, or rough. I wanted to take away all distraction from the movement, and from Chris's work—from the way their muscles moved, their grace, the way that their hands touched. It was so beautiful the way that they moved and touched. It was so sensual. I wanted to capture that, and the way those fingertips touched each other. I kept saying half-jokingly, "They should be naked."

CHRISTOPHER: They were wearing something, but there was a certain excitement, too—especially at the beginning, when the two girls are wearing shifts. The guy runs his hands up the body, and just pulls the little shift up above the panty line. And they've got this beautiful flesh, but the leotard's on underneath. For a second, it's like a gasp. It's not shocking, but it just makes everyone's heart beat a little bit faster.

BETSY: Narciso, how do you describe the costumes you created for the ballet?

NARCISO: The costumes have some of my signature touches—such as the particular seams that I've used—and there are other details that are always present in my work … but they're slightly different in my other work. These were built for athletes, and used in a very different way.

CHRISTOPHER: Outstanding is the way that I describe them. There was something that felt like a strange kind of community of fairies. It's a very bizarre thing to say, but I think the overall feeling of the piece was of people emerging from some kind of magical place, because of the subtlety of the color, the pale pinks and flesh tones. And everything seems a little translucent.

BETSY: Maybe ethereal?

CHRISTOPHER: Yes.

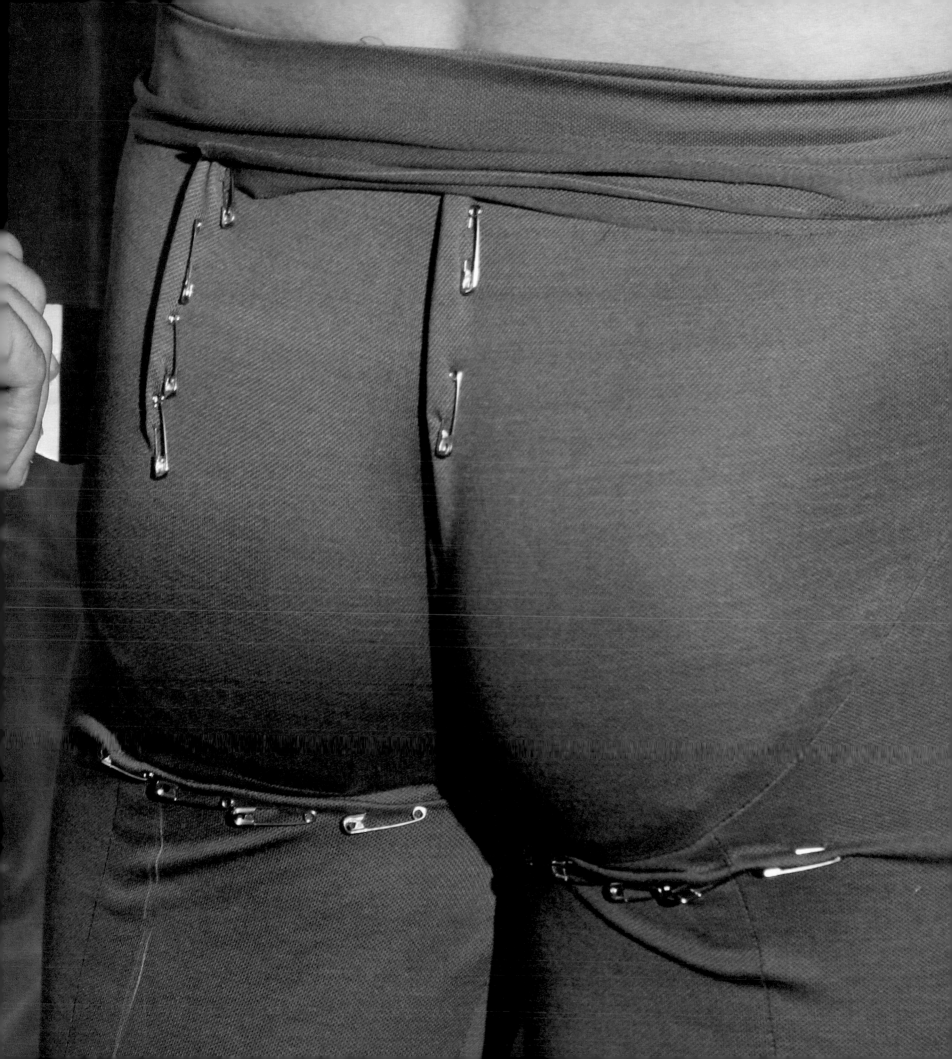

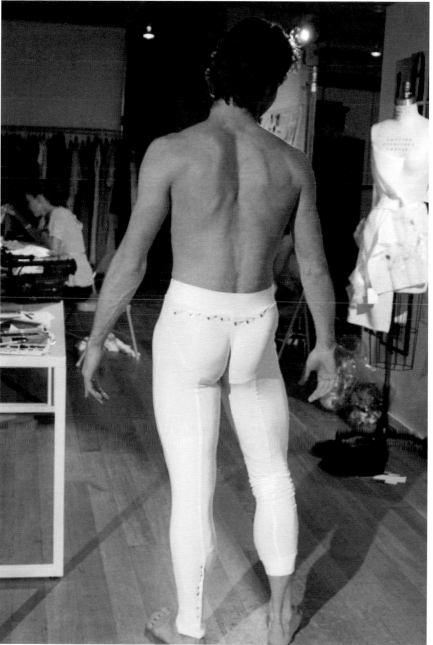

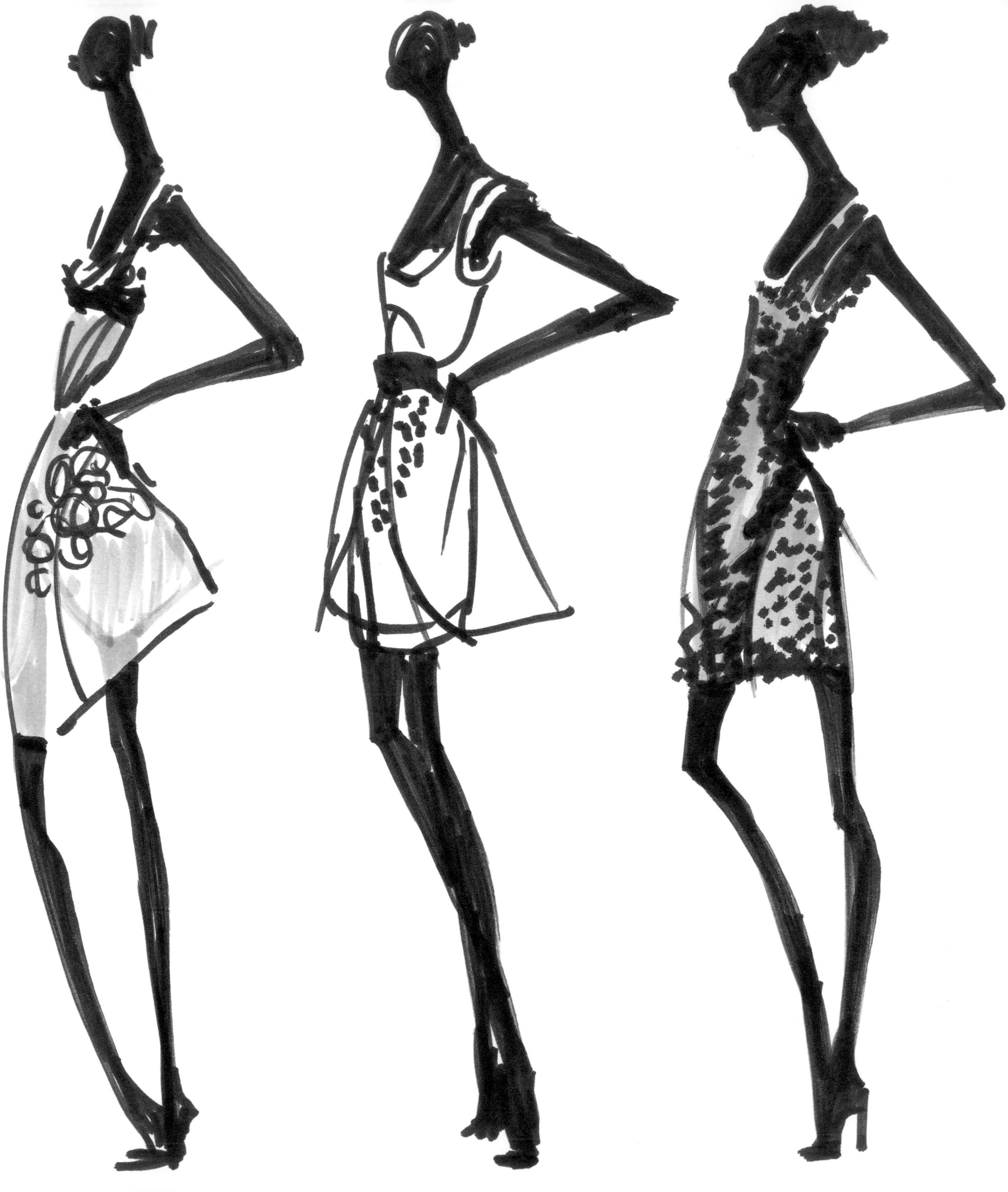

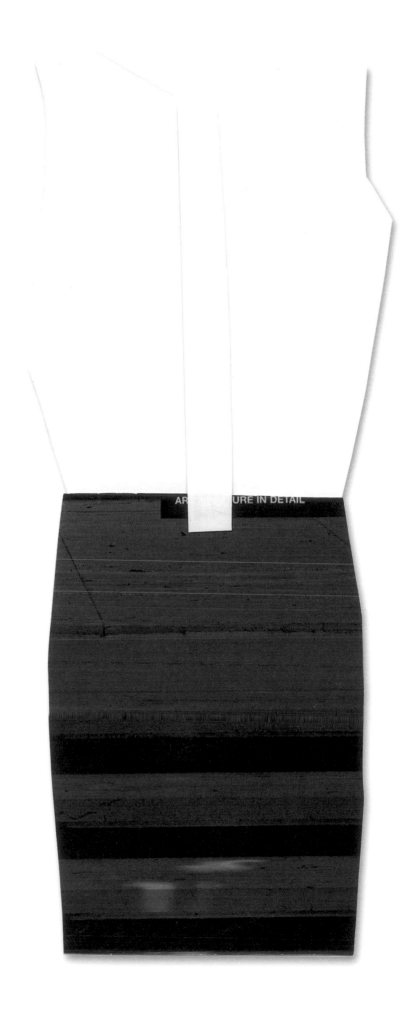

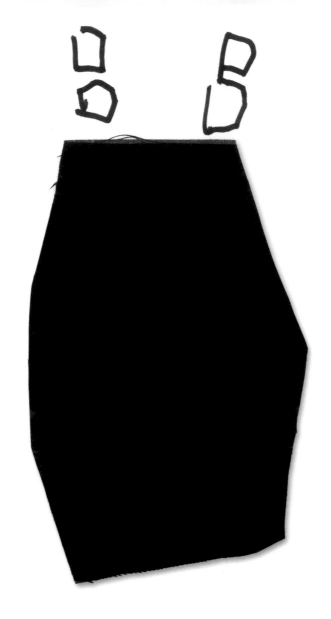

Real
Dress

W/ RAW
BONES e/f

emb

Real
Dress

Narciso Rodriguez in conversation with Ruben and Isabel Toledo

NARCISO: Did you get to see the Madame Grès exhibit?

ISABEL: Yes! We went to the opening.

RUBEN: Beautiful.

NARCISO: I would've loved to have the experience of seeing the exhibit with you both. Her work was truly unique.

ISABEL: Yes, her technique and her ability to manipulate the fabric are really incredible. It's like a mathematical equation in her hands. And with jersey, you really have to be so precise.

RUBEN: She was definitely a mathematician.

ISABEL: You can see it. I can look at her work and tell Ruben exactly the way she engineered it, how she cut the pattern.

RUBEN: That's because you think the same way she did. You have such a mathematical mind, too. [*To Narciso*] Isabel can see a puzzle and point to how the pieces fit together and say, "Oh, well that's this and this is that."

ISABEL: Narciso, what was your favorite piece?

NARCISO: The dress I loved the most was the white crepe gown at the entrance that seemed to be based on a classic shirt dress, except it had a deep plunge and peplum in front. It was quite delicate and classic, yet extremely modern in its cut and transparency. It was so simple and pure and made with such exquisite craftsmanship. It was wearable and sexy *and* beautiful. I tried to imagine the history behind it: how Grès might have made it, who might have worn it, and *where* they might have worn it. Then inside the exhibit, there was another dress, a ruffle collar gown made in a blackish green faille. It was massive, yet so graceful.

ISABEL: Such stark contrast.

NARCISO: I found them so unusual and not what I think of as Grès at all.

ISABEL: Yes, I know. One usually only thinks of jersey and draping.

NARCISO: There was also a nude piece with a cascade down the front that was on the cover of the invitation. It was classic Grès, unbelievably precise!

ISABEL: She was a master of her craft.

NARCISO: That show was impressive because I saw so much about the history of fashion—all kinds of techniques—and what also made it interesting was that Grès has never been the most celebrated

designer, yet we see so much of what we know now about fashion in her work, way before people discovered those techniques. There were many pieces that were way ahead of their time. They reminded me of Halston or Zoran and, again, they were not what you expected from Grès. Pure, clean shapes that showed what a true genius she was and how she influenced countless designers.

RUBEN: The way she worked was also very seductive . . .

NARCISO: That's interesting, I've never thought of her work as being that seductive because there is so much structure underneath . . .

RUBEN: True, but it *looks* soft and sensual.

NARCISO: As if it's molding the body instead of the body giving it the shape.

ISABEL: The fabric use is *so* sensitive, all that fine silk jersey . . .

NARCISO: It *is* a lot of silk jersey . . . where can you find that fabric? Who makes that today? [*laughs*] It made me think of you a lot, Isabel, because of the way you work.

ISABEL: Well, in the way *we* work . . .

NARCISO: It's always so stimulating to see something through someone else's eyes. Again, it's why I wished I'd seen the show with you. When you bring someone new into the creative process, it makes you think so differently.

ISABEL: We totally know that.

NARCISO: You are so lucky because you have each other to—

RUBEN: To open each other's eyes.

NARCISO: Those relationships are so important to a designer or artist. Yours is unique. There is nothing like what you two share.

RUBEN: I thought everybody worked this way.

NARCISO: No. It rarely exists.

ISABEL: We really do work on everything together . . . And it does make all the difference.

RUBEN: I have to say I'm spoiled.

NARCISO: When I look at your illustrations, Ruben, I see something that's somehow romantic without being fussy, like what I imagine Cuba to have been. I envision a courtyard and a house in Havana with beautiful wrought iron. It is also the way I see Cuban women— very dignified, very strong, like a type of wrought-iron lacework.

RUBEN: But that's definitely Isabel! She is in everything I do. I only began to understand what Cuba was really about when I met her, because I was the only Cuban kid where I grew up. Although when I think about it, I do have memories of wrought iron and incredible places in Havana. I remember an aura of balconies and windows . . . and lots of shadows. It was such a great city for shadows. I've never forgotten those shadows; they could be really creepy or really beautiful.

NARCISO: I love photographing shadows.

ISABEL: It must be in the DNA . . .

NARCISO: I was very lucky growing up in an area in New Jersey that was mixed: Portuguese, Spaniards, African Americans. There was also a large Italian community in that area—and of course, Cubans. So you would go to all the picnics and the baseball games and the cookouts— and there were always these big Cuban dances at the park.

ISABEL: How would you define Cuban?

RUBEN: Warm, social, and welcoming. Everyone is invited in. It's very inclusive. Food, of course, is first and foremost. Then music. Ul- timately though, it's the warmth and pride of the people that shines through, don't you think?

NARCISO: Growing up in that very loud kind of environment—I would be astonished by the noise level. You'd have a table full of people, and everybody's talking at the same time—

ISABEL: People talking over each other. It's unbelievable.

RUBEN: But they're not distracted, they're still very focused. They still say what they feel, which I think is a very Cuban thing.

NARCISO: I'm not typically Cuban in that I'm pretty quiet and low- key. I retreated into my art even as a kid.

ISABEL: But your father's very Cuban . . .

NARCISO: Yes, I really admire his strength. My parents came here when they were very young, in the mid-fifties, to start a family. It was before the revolution, so they weren't fleeing anything. They didn't speak English and they didn't have any money. They were very coura- geous, very brave. I didn't recognize that until I was an adult. I always tell my dad that what he did was so much more courageous than I could ever do. I've had opportunities to work in Europe and commute. And I don't do it because it's so difficult to be away from home. What they did was really hard-core. It wasn't like now, where you can just take a jet and see your relatives and friends in a few hours. You look at their old pictures from Cuba, with everybody around the table and all the cousins and the aunts and uncles—they just left all that behind.

RUBEN: Your father is a very special guy.

NARCISO: He really is. Everybody loves him. He's just very open, very warm . . .

ISABEL: And the sweetest guy you'll ever meet—that smile! For me, as a kid in Cuba, what I loved most was the presence of music and dancing everywhere, indoors, outdoors . . . It was exhilarating. When Ruben and I got to collaborate with Twyla Tharp on a Cuban dance project, we were so thrilled.

NARCISO: When? How did I miss that?

RUBEN: In 1998, we worked on a ballet with her. She's amazing to work with. Talk about focus and drive.

NARCISO: That is something that I would have loved to have seen.

ISABEL: How was your experience with Chris Wheeldon's ballet?

NARCISO: Working with dancers is extraordinary. It was also a little scary at first because I kept thinking, *Is something going to fall out*?

ISABEL: [*laughs*]

NARCISO: Watching the rehearsals, speaking to Chris and the dancers, seeing how athletic and graceful they were, truly inspired the work I did for them. The idea of working with Cuban dancers would be cool. Maybe that should be a project we can work on together?

ISABEL: Oh, I would love that!

NARCISO: I'm always drawn to Cuban women. They have such strong personalities and such strength of character and femininity.

RUBEN: Absolutely. I can attest to that.

ISABEL: Well, I come from a family of women. My mom had fifteen sisters and three brothers so it's a huge female family.

NARCISO: Fifteen sisters? When I think of all the incredible women I was exposed to growing up Cuban . . . it left such a profound impression. Their personalities were larger than life, and you grew up with sixteen of them, including your mother! [*laughs*]

ISABEL: They were multifaceted and I admired them all. I'd like to think that I'm like them.

NARCISO: I've met very few women like you, Isabel. You have a very special gift.

RUBEN: I have to agree.

NARCISO: I look at you and I'm reminded of all the great Cuban women I've known and been inspired by. I had the opportunity to dress Celia Cruz, one of the most spectacular Cuban women of all time. She was so gracious and warm and really personified the dignity, the pride, and the grace of Cuban women, as do you, Isabel.

ISABEL: Wow! Thank you.

RUBEN: I'm a very lucky man!

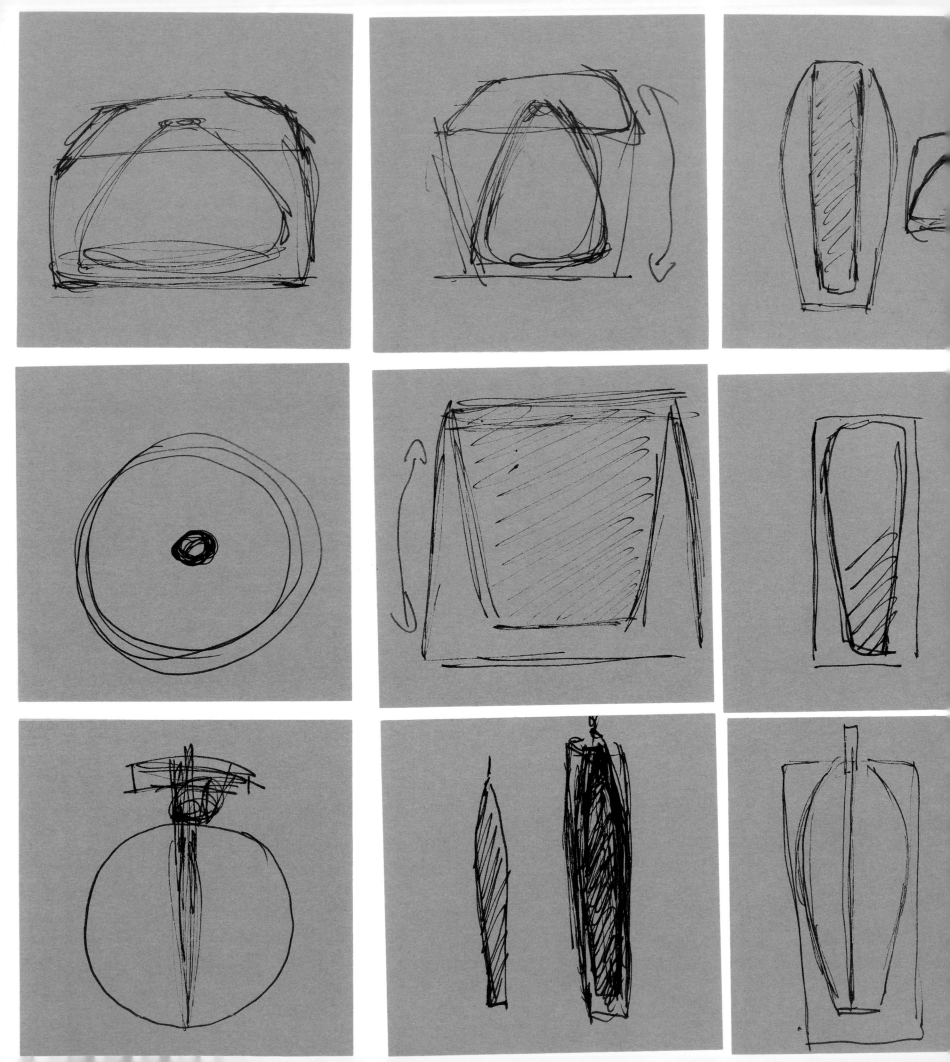

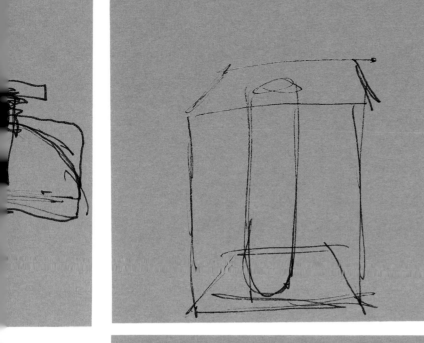

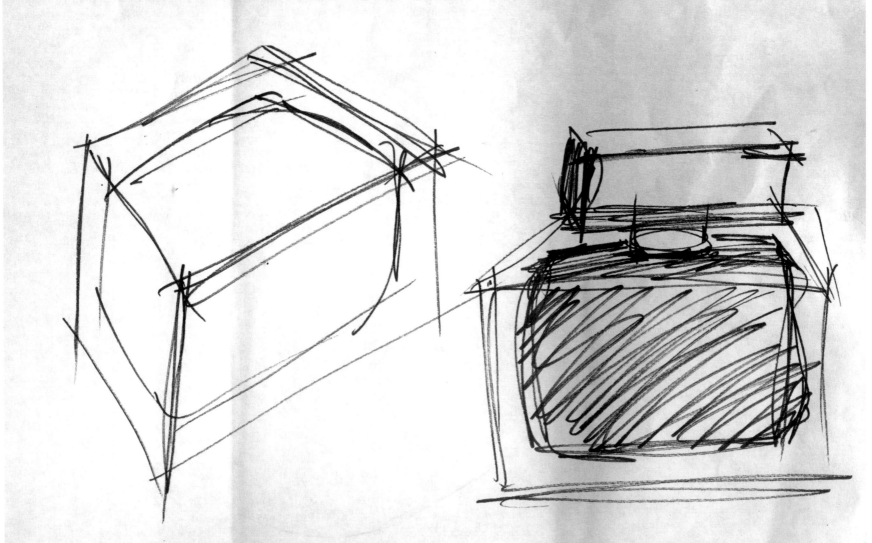

Acknowledgments

Special thanks to Danny Pfeffer for editing this book and to Betsy Berne, Cathy Horyn, Cindy Sherman, Ruben and Isabel Toledo, Caetano Veloso, Rachel Weisz, and Christopher Wheeldon for their conversations.

Charles Miers, Ilaria Fusina, Anthony Petrillose, Maria Pia Gramaglia, and Minnie Weisz at Rizzoli. Creative Director Sam Shahid and Art Director Matt Kraus at Shahid and Company for their design and direction.

Photographers Erin Baiano, Richard Ballard, Mario Canivello, Noel Federizo, Mitchell Feinberg, Greg Kadel, Francesco Lagnese, Annie Leibovitz, Jacky Marshall, Craig McDean, The Estate of James Moore, Peter Riesett, Frances Roberts, Alexis Rodriguez-Duarte, Yaniv Schulman, Ingrid Solomonson, Mario Testino, Inez van Lamsweerde and Vinoodh Matadin, Ben Watts, and Anthony Ward for contributing their images.

Lisa Muscatel, Kathy Kalesti, Simon Holloway, Brenda Mikel, Mei Zou, Lindsay Hamlin, Simone Leonhardt, Sumie Yamashita, LeighAnne Vitullo, Casey Cadwallader, Julien David, and Jo-Anne Rossell for their support. My parents, Pierre Rougier and PR Consulting, Darren Aronofsky, Carolina Bittencourt, Zach Carr, Lori Goldstein, Svetlana Ivanovna, KCD, Donna Karan, Calvin Klein, Blanca Lasalle, Paula Lavigne, Doug Lloyd, M&M, Beate Moore, Camilla Nickerson, Dick Page, Sarah Jessica Parker, Silvia Pintor, Orlando Pita, Jerry, Jessica, Sascha, Juju, and Shepy Seinfeld, Sally Singer, Eugene Souleiman, Giovanni Testino, Sasha Vaigichev, Melanie Ward, Jessica Weinstein, Anna Wintour, the many agencies who help us each season and the models who appear in this book, graffiti artists around the world and the people of Brazil.

And especially to Rémy Gomez, Léa Vignal Kenedi, BPI, and all the muses.

Captions / Credits

FRONT & BACK COVERS: Spring 2008 fittings photographed by Narciso Rodriguez ENDPAPER: Covers of Narciso's sketchbooks photographed by Peter Riesett PAGE 1: Narciso's hands photographed by Jacky Marshall PAGE 6: "Narciso Rodriguez" by Betsy Berne PAGE 7: Narciso photographed by Inez van Lamsweerde and Vinoodh Matadin for *V Magazine* PAGE 12: Fitting photographed by Narciso Rodriguez PAGE 12–13: Resort 2009 collages by Narciso Rodriguez photographed by Peter Riesett PAGE 14: Photograph by Jacky Marshall PAGE 15: Christy Turlington in Spring 2002 shot for *Harper's Bazaar* by Greg Kadel; illustration by Narciso Rodriguez PAGES 16–17: Fall 2008 fittings photographed by Yaniv Schulman PAGE 18: Fall 2000 shoes photographed for Italian *Vogue* by James

Moore PAGE 19: Illustration by Narciso Rodriguez; photographs of Brazil sunset by Narciso Rodriguez PAGES 20–21: Brazil sky and kites photographed by Narciso Rodriguez PAGES 22–23: Jennifer Lopez wearing Spring 2005 photographed for American *Vogue* by Mario Testino/Art Partner PAGE 24: Illustration by Narciso Rodriguez photographed by Peter Riesett PAGE 25: Left, glass on street photographed by Narciso Rodriguez; right, Karen Elson in Fall 2000 photographed for *Harper's Bazaar* © Craig McDean/Art + Commerce PAGES 26–27: Inspiration wall for Spring 2008 PAGE 28: Shoe from the Spring 2005 collection PAGE 29: Fall 2006 fitting photographed by Lisa Muscatel PAGES 30–31: Sketches from the Spring 2008 collection by Narciso Rodriguez photographed by Peter Riesett PAGES 32–33: Sketches by Narciso Rodriguez PAGES 34–35: Sketches by Narciso Rodriguez; photographs of Astor Place by Narciso Rodriguez PAGE 36: Woman on 14th Street and Third Avenue photographed by Narciso Rodriguez   PAGE 37: Illustrations by Narciso Rodriguez   PAGE 38: Shoe sketch by Narciso Rodriguez   PAGE 39: Top, photograph by Jacky Marshall; bottom, photograph taken backstage at the Fall 2000 show by Richard Ballard   PAGES 40–41: Sketches by Narciso Rodriguez   PAGES 42–43: Fall 2005 fitting photographed by Jacky Marshall   PAGE 44: Flavia de Oliveira in Spring 2007 photographed for *Harper's Bazaar* by Anthony Ward/Art Partner   PAGE 45: Inspiration for Spring 2007; *Star Wars*, race cars and a waitress in San Mauro Pascoli, Italy   PAGES 46–47: Fabrics for Spring 2007   PAGE 48: Fall 2001 photographed by Richard Ballard   PAGES 49–50: Fittings for Spring and Fall 2005 photographed by Jacky Marshall   PAGE 51: Corrections on a jacket from Spring 2008   PAGES 52–53: Fitting photographed by Jacky Marshall   PAGES 54–56: Inspiration found on the streets of Brazil, drawn and photographed by Narciso Rodriguez   PAGES 57–59: Spring 2008 fittings

photographed by Narciso Rodriguez   PAGES 60–61: A flash of Fall 1998 photographed by Narciso Rodriguez   PAGES 62–63: Spring 2008 fittings photographed by Narciso Rodriguez   PAGE 64: Spring 2007 fitting photographed by Narciso Rodriguez   PAGE 65: Spring 2008 fittings photographed by Narciso Rodriguez   PAGES 66–67: Fabric collages for Fall 2007 by Narciso Rodriguez photographed by Peter Riesett   PAGE 69: Sarah Jessica Parker in Fall 2005 photographed for American *Vogue* by Annie Leibovitz/Contact Press Images   PAGES 70–73: Sun reflections inspire fabric patterns for Fall 2007   PAGES 74–78: Fittings photographed by Narciso Rodriguez   PAGE 79: Top left photograph by Yaniv Schulman; all others by Narciso Rodriguez   PAGES 80–81: Illustrations for Fall 2007 by Narciso Rodriguez   PAGES 82–89: Brazilian graffiti and the beach are constant sources of inspiration. All photographs by Narciso Rodriguez   PAGE 90: A look from Spring 2008 photographed by Monica Feudi   PAGE 91: The black sand beaches of Tenerife, Canary Islands inspire embroideries **PAGES 92–93:** Salvador, in Brazil's Bahia region, provides inspiration for color and texture **PAGES 94–97:** Photographs by Narciso Rodriguez **PAGE 97:** Backstage Fall 2005 photographed by Jacky Marshall **PAGE 98:** Backstage Spring 2004 photographed by Jacky Marshall **PAGE 99:** Clouds photographed by Narciso Rodriguez **PAGE 100:** "Art, Sex, and Wrinkles: A Conversation with Cindy Sherman," by Cathy Horyn **PAGE 101:** Cindy Sherman photographed by Cindy Sherman, *Untitled Film Still #56,* 1980, black-and-white photograph courtesy of the artist and Metro Pictures. **PAGES 106–107:** A New Jersey scene photographed by Narciso Rodriguez **PAGE 108:** Kate Moss in Fall 2001 being photographed for an ad in the East Village of New York City **PAGES 109–111:** Architecture and life on the street form the inspiration for fabric texture and design **PAGES 112–115:** Fall 2004 fittings photographed by Jacky Marshall **PAGES 116–117:** Street life

photographed by Narciso Rodriguez **PAGES 118–119:** Shadows of scaffolding inspires Spring 2003: left, photo by Richard Ballard; right, Narciso Rodriguez **PAGE 120:** Sketch of Fall 2007 gown by Narciso Rodriguez photographed by Peter Riesett **PAGE 121:** Gown embroidery details for Fall 2007 **PAGES 122–123:** Sarah Jessica Parker wearing Fall 2008 photographed with Chris Noth for American *Vogue* by Annie Leibovitz/Contact Press Images **PAGES 124–125:** Inspiration wall for the Fall 2004 collection photographed by Frances M. Roberts **PAGES 126–127:** Fitting Daria Werbowy for Fall 2004 photographed by Jacky Marshall **PAGE 128:** Sketches by Narciso Rodriguez **PAGE 129:** Backstage at the Spring 2003 show photographed by Richard Ballard **PAGES 130–131:** Evaluating a look from Spring 2004 photographed by Jacky Marshall **PAGE 133:** Uma Thurman photographed in Spring 2004 for American *Vogue* by Annie Leibovitz/Contact Press Images **PAGES 134–135:** Fabric collages for

Fall 2007 by Narciso Rodriguez photographed by Peter Riesett PAGES 136–139: Inspiration and fabric collages from Spring 2007 photographed by Peter Riesett PAGE 139: Right, backstage at the Spring 2004 collection photographed by Jacky Marshall PAGE 140: Polaroids taken of friends PAGE 141: Narciso Rodriguez and Sarah Jessica Parker in Spring 2004 photographed for American *Vogue* by Noel Federizo PAGES 142–143: Graffiti wall in Rio de Janeiro photographed by Narciso Rodriguez PAGES 144–145: Kickboxing photographed off the television inspires Spring 2007 PAGES 146–147: Sketches from Spring 2005 PAGES 148–149: Architecture in Italy photographed by Narciso inspires Spring 2003, photographed backstage by Richard Ballard PAGES 150–151: Sketches of people on the street by Narciso Rodriguez PAGES 152–155: Movement and light on Ipanema Beach, Rio de Janeiro, Brazil, photographed by Narciso Rodriguez PAGE 156: Narciso Rodriguez in conversation with Caetano Veloso PAGE 157:

Singer and composer Caetano Veloso wearing Oiticica's *P 04 Parangolé Cape 01*, 1964 in 1968. © Projeto Hélio Oiticica. Photographer unknown. PAGE 158–159: Hélio Oiticica with Bólides and Parangolés in his studio in Rio de Janeiro, c.1965. © Projeto Hélio Oiticica. Photo: Desdemone Bardin PAGE 160: Narciso Rodriguez in Salvador, in Brazil's Bahia region, photographed by Mário Canivello PAGES 162–163: Carnival in Rio de Janeiro photographed by Narciso Rodriguez PAGES 164–165: New York sky photographed by Narciso Rodriguez PAGES 166–171: Spring 2008 fittings photographed by Narciso Rodriguez PAGES 172–173: A photograph taken by Narciso of a child's birthday party inspires colors for Spring 2008 PAGES 174: Self-portrait during a late-night fitting by Narciso Rodriguez PAGES 175–177: Spring 2008 fittings photographed by Narciso Rodriguez PAGES 178–179: Draping Spring 2006 photographed by Jacky Marshall PAGES 180–181: Spring 2008 sketched and photographed by Narciso

Rodriguez PAGES 182–183: Fabric collages for Spring 2007 by Narciso Rodriguez photographed by Peter Riesett PAGES 184–187: Inspiration wall for Spring 2007 PAGES 188–191: The East Village of New York City photographed by Narciso Rodriguez PAGES 192–193: Sketches of people on the street by Narciso Rodriguez PAGES 194–197: People on the street are a constant source of inspiration, photographed by Narciso Rodriguez PAGES 198–199: Photographs taken in Italy by Narciso Rodriguez inspire color and texture PAGE 200: Narciso Rodriguez in conversation with Rachel Weisz PAGES 202–203: Narciso Rodriguez and Rachel Weisz photographed for the *New York Times* by Ben Watts/Corbis Outline PAGES 206–207: Photographs of Carolyn Bessette by Jacky Marshall PAGE 208: Narciso Rodriguez in coversation with Christopher Wheldon PAGES 210–211: Christopher Wheeldon rehearsing his dancers for Prokofiev's pas de deux, photographed by Yaniv Schulman PAGE 212: Fittings for Morphoses, clockwise from top left: Adrian Danchig-Waring photographed by Narciso Rodriguez; *Fool's Paradise* photographed by Erin Baiano; Maria Kowroski photographed by Narciso Rodriguez; Adrian Danchig-Waring, Teresa Reichlen, and Jared Angle from *Fool's Paradise* photographed by Erin Baiano; Adrian Danchig-Waring, Teresa Reichlen, and Jared Angle from *Fool's Paradise* photographed by Erin Baiano; Gonzalo Garcia, Craig Hall and Aesha Ash from *Fool's Paradise* photographed by Erin Balano. PAGE 213: Ballet sketch by Narciso Rodriguez PAGES 214–215: Ballet fitting for *Fool's Paradise* photographed by Yaniv Schulman PAGE 216: Inspiration wall PAGE 217: Gonzalo Garcia photographed by Narciso Rodriguez PAGES 218–219: The movement of a raincoat provides inspiration photographed by Narciso Rodriguez PAGES 220–221: Jacky Marshall, Donna Karan, and Narciso Rodriguez photographed by Ingrid Solomonson PAGES 222–223: Sketches of Spring 2008 by Narciso

Rodriguez PAGE 225: Milana Keller photographed by Lisa Muscatel PAGES 226–229: Farnsworth House collages by Narciso Rodriguez PAGES 230–231: Fabric collages of Spring 2007 by Narciso Rodriguez photographed by Peter Riesett PAGE 232: Narciso Rodriguez in coversation with Isabel and Ruben Toledo PAGE 233: Illustration of Narciso Rodriguez by Ruben Toledo PAGE 236: Illustration of Isabel Toledo and Narciso Rodriguez by Ruben Toledo PAGES 238–239: Celia Cruz being fitted by Narciso Rodriguez photographed by Alexis Rodriguez-Duarte PAGE 241: Narciso Rodriguez fitting Celia Cruz photographed by Francesco Lagnese PAGE 242: Carmen Kass photographed by Inez van Lamsweerde and Vinoodh Matadin PAGE 243: Illustrations by Narciso Rodriguez; For Her fragrance photographed by Inez van Lamsweerde and Vinoodh Matadin PAGES 244–245: Fragrance bottle sketches by Narciso Rodriguez PAGE 246: For Him fragrance bottle photographed by Inez van Lamsweerde and Vinoodh Matadin; bottle sketches by Narciso Rodriguez PAGE 247: Evandro Soldati photographed by Inez van Lamsweerde and Vinoodh Matadin PAGES 248–250: Backstage at the Spring 2006 show photographed by Jacky Marshall PAGE 251: Backstage at the Spring 2004 show photographed by Jacky Marshall PAGES 252–253: Backstage at the Spring 1998 show, Narciso's first collection under his own label, photographed by Richard Ballard PAGES 254–255: Backstage at the Spring 2004 show photographed by Jacky Marshall PAGES 256–257: Backstage at the Spring 1998 show photographed by Richard Ballard PAGE 258–259: Narciso Rodriguez photographed backstage at the Fall 2003 show by Richard Ballard PAGES 262–263: Graffiti wall in Rio de Janeiro by Marcos Wark photographed by Narciso Rodriguez PAGE 271: Backstage at the Spring 1998 show photographed by Richard Ballard

First published in the United States of America in 2008

by Rizzoli International Publications, Inc.

300 Park Avenue South

New York, NY 10010

www.rizzoliusa.com

DESIGN BY SAM SHAHID

2008 2009 2010 2011 / 10 9 8 7 6 5 4 3 2 1

Distributed in the U.S. trade by Random House, New York

Printed in China

ISBN 13: 978-0-8478-3141-8

Library of Congress Catalog Control Number: 2008932396